IAN ALLAN PUBLISHING
ISBN 978-0-7110-3509-6
£16.99
WWW.IANALLAN
PUBLISHING.CO.UK

The Elephant Never Forgot

London's Trams in Retrospect

Paul Collins

This book takes a slightly different approach to covering London's trams from George Train's experiments in the 1860s to the Croydon Tramlink and other recent proposals. The book covers the background to the setting up of the various London tramway companies, technical details of their building and operation, including a detailed look at all facets of the Kingsway Subway, publicity and improvements to the system and the vehicles used, notably experimental tramcar LCC No 1, the campaign to save London's trams, plus discussion of trams on film including, of course, the London Transport film 'The Elephant Will Never Forget', which offers the book its title. There are plenty of pictures of trams and street scenes, but against a background of how they came to be there and how much they were missed by those who had used them.

The Elephant Never Forgot
London's Trams in Retrospect

Paul Collins

The Elephant Never Forgot

London's Trams in Retrospect
Paul Collins

Ian Allan Publishing • *Printed Paper Cased*
235 x 172mm • *96 pages* •
978 0 7110 3509 6 • *£16.99*

- A comprehensive album examining the development, structure and operation of London's trams from the 1860s onwards.
- The follow up to author Paul Collins first book, this volume looks at several new areas which give further insights into the development and operation of London trams from the 1860s to the current Croydon Tramlink.

The Elephant Never Forgot

London's Trams in Retrospect

Paul Collins

Ian Allan PUBLISHING

First published 2010

ISBN 978 0 7110 3509 6

Published by Ian Allan Publishing

an imprint of Ian Allan Publishing Ltd, Hersham,
Surrey, KT12 4RG
Printed in England by Ian Allan Printing Ltd, Hersham,
Surrey, KT12 4RG

Code: 1010/B1

Distributed in the United States of America and Canada
by BookMasters Distribution Services

Visit the Ian Allan Publishing website at www.ianallanpublishing.com

Contents

Introduction

As well as the Olympics, 2012 will mark the 60th anniversary of the closure of London's first generation of electric trams. Those who remember the trams will, of necessity, be of advancing years and their memories will be of ageing cars working on a contracted system, slated for closure and labouring under a backlog of deferred maintenance. Those nostalgic for trams they never saw have, in the main, to rely upon the films, photographs and recordings made during the trams' final years. However, there is a wealth of material, contemporary to all points in London's tramway history, which can pare away the intervening years and show things how they were. That is what this book is about.

London's first trams came to the capital courtesy of the ambition of a flamboyant American entrepreneur with a slightly inappropriate surname — George Francis Train. That he had three demonstration lines running in the capital between 1861 and 1862 is well known; less appreciated is the fact that he first tried to lay down a line right in the heart of the city. The furore this stirred up tells us much about the prevailing attitudes of the times and hints at why later tramway schemes failed to penetrate the capital's centre.

In its latter years London's tram system was basically a reduced version of the former LCC network and, with a notable exception, worked by the County Council's old cars, plus similar ones inherited from smaller local authority systems. Missing were the routes and vehicles from the tramways built by private companies. How these lines came about is a story of great persistence and enterprise, which also reflects the personality of two electrical and tramway pioneers: the London United Tramways' James Clifton Robinson and the Metropolitan Electric Tramways' Emile Garcke. The story also embraces that of the South Metropolitan Electric Tramways & Lighting Co Ltd, which found that, in order to build a street tramway, it was sometimes necessary first to build the street!

Through its adoption of the conduit system of current collection, the LCC Tramways accepted more complex engineering than any other operator in the capital. It did not shy away from such things and also overcame formidable difficulties to construct a tramway subway, with tracks at times 34ft below street level. Texts written for tramway, railway and general engineering students reveal how this was done.

Maintaining and repairing a large fleet of tramcars was no mean feat. All of London's tramway operators did this one way or another, but only the LCC built a special facility for the purpose — the Central Repair Works at Charlton. Articles from the technical and trade press at the time this opened show how it was designed and operated.

When newly maintained and out-shopped from the Central Repair Works, the LCC's trams were very eye-catching. Equally so was the publicity material — leaflets, posters, snappy copy on the back of tickets — with which they were promoted. These striking designs were often the work of up and coming artists who went on to enjoy illustrious careers.

Although to the casual observer most of London's tramcars looked very similar, they were built over a period of a quarter of a century or so. The last cars ordered by the LCC took advantage of new construction methods and advances in equipment, which made them as modern as any others plying the capital's streets at the time, as the trade press of the time reported.

As well as recording London's passing trams on film and tape, some enthusiasts campaigned for their retention and modernisation. Through the collected papers of one such individual something of the detail and intelligence of this campaign emerges.

Today's multimedia age makes both still and moving images readily available to view at home. This includes those of London trams in their prime. Their most famous filmed record is the British Transport Films documentary *The Elephant Will Never Forget*, the story behind the making of which is almost as fascinating as the film itself.

May 2000 saw the return of trams to London in the form of Tramlink in Croydon. Buoyed by its success, a number of tram schemes were promoted, but despite extensive planning and consultation none of them now looks likely to materialise.

Acknowledgements

I am extremely grateful to everyone whose work is seen on these pages or who helped me in any way in preparing this book. In particular I would like to thank the following for their time and trouble: the British Film Institute, Nick Catford, June Collins, Paul Cripps, Ray Cresswell and Brierley Printing, Nick Grant, Mellanie Hartland, Ian Allan Publishing Ltd, Ironbridge Gorge Museum Trust, Jack Law, London's Transport Museum, Simon Murphy, Patrick Russell and Peter Waller.

Paul Collins
Wollaston, Stourbridge
April 2010

1. 'Putting a temptation in the way of the lower classes …'
George Francis Train and the 'fever' in Marylebone

The American George Francis Train, who had made a fortune from clipper ships by his late 20s, introduced street tramways to the UK. He had first seen them in Philadelphia in the late 1850s and immediately recognised their potential. Equally quickly, Train also saw Europe as a market ripe for street tramways. He arrived in Liverpool early in 1860 and, having failed in an attempt to lay down a demonstration line there, made approaches to the authorities in Birkenhead in March 1860. These met with success and on 30 August 1860 he opened a 1¼-mile horse tramway line between Woodside Ferry and Birkenhead Park. This was an able demonstration, but his ambitions lay elsewhere, as he wrote in 1860: 'When I made up my mind last year to succeed in demonstrating the practicability of these railways in English cities, London was the starting point …'

To this end, Train published a pamphlet, 'Observations on Street Railways', which was addressed to the Rt Hon Milner Gibson MP, President of the Board of Trade, the document being a form of 'petition' for permission to conduct a trial, as at Birkenhead, in London. Simultaneously, Train began to seek permission to lay down a demonstration line in the heart of London, along streets within the Parish of St Marylebone.

Their deliberations were recorded verbatim and stand as a testament to the prevailing attitudes of those in authority in mid-Victorian London when faced with technology and innovation, which they (perhaps) did not fully understand. This is from Train's original application to the Marylebone Vestry Committee, dated 9 August 1860: 'I am desirous of further demonstrating the system by a trial line in London. I hereby apply for permission to lay down a line from the northern boundary of the parish, in the Finchley Road, along that road, the Wellington Road, Park Road, Upper Baker Street, York Place, Baker Street, east side of Portman Square, Edwards Street, Wigmore Street, north side of Cavendish Square, Cavendish Place, Regent Street, to Oxford Street, returning by Oxford Street, Portman Street, west side of Portman Square, along the line of Gloucester Street and Gloucester Place; a second return line to the boundary of the parish in Finchley Road, and to join the route already named in Park Road. The whole to be done at my cost, in a way satisfactory to your Surveyor.'

George Francis Train (24 March 1829 – 5 January 1904) was an American entrepreneur who introduced street tramways to Britain. He is seen here in a photographic *carte de visite* produced about the time he was wooing the authorities in Liverpool and London to allow him to conduct his experiments in 'street railways'. *Author's collection*

The Vestry resolved to refer this application to the Metropolitan Subterranean Railway Committee then sitting — for them to report to the Vestry thereon'. The following week the Committee held a special meeting and, after mature deliberation, framed a report, which, however, could not be submitted to the Vestry until six weeks afterwards, in consequence of the adjournment of the Vestry having taken place *ad interim* for the annual vacation.

The committee recommended the adoption of Train's proposal, and the matter was discussed at the weekly meeting of the Representative Council of the Parish of St Marylebone, held at the Court House, Marylebone Lane, on Saturday 6 October 1860.

Before the meeting could address Train's application the proceedings were effectively interrupted by a deputation from the directors of the London General Omnibus Company who 'desired an interview with the Vestry, on the subject of street railways'. They referred to a letter they had submitted on 3 October 1860 which cited an application they had made in 1857/8 to lay down a street railway in the parish, which the Vestry had rejected 'to the effect that the scheme would be fraught with the greatest danger to the lives and limbs of the public, and impede the public traffic'. They then, in effect, cried foul, stating that 'My directors have therefore seen, with much surprise, the favourable reception now given to the proposals of Mr Train,' and requested the Vestry to defer its decision until they had submitted their plans.

Curiously, the Vestry had also received a letter from William Curtis, dated 5 October 1860, in which he proposed 'exhibiting to the Vestry the original carriage, which has been at work for some time upon the railway along the line of Docks at Liverpool. The peculiarity of my system is, that the carriages, by means of moveable flanges applied to the wheels, are adapted to run both on the rail and common road, and are transferred from the rail to the road and *vice versa* at any moment with perfect facility, at the will of the driver; and when upon the rail, the carriages are as safe as an ordinary railway carriage. The object of my invention is to overcome the objection to the necessity of the "right of way", which must be acceded to in other mode of railway locomotion (and which is especially necessary in the American system advocated by Mr Train). The conveyance keeps the rails as long as there is no obstacle to their progress, but should an obstacle occur, it is avoided with as much facility as by carriages working along the granite trams laid along many of the ordinary streets of the metropolis. This line of trams will suffice for two lines of traffic, excepting where the traffic is very great … At Liverpool, the "Enterprise" was at work with perfect success in May and June of last year, and other carriages on the same principle are daily at work along the same line and crowded streets of that town, without imperilling or being impeded either with the railway and the ordinary traffic of the street. Passengers, carriages, and horses cross the rails at any angle with perfect facility and safety.

G. F. Train's proposed lines in the Parish of St Marylebone, shown on a map produced in 1858. South of the point where the lines divided they would have been single and one way; north of this point they would have been double. Had these lines been built they would have been both the first one-way and the first double tramlines ever laid in this country. *Author's collection*

With the permission of the Commissioners of the Metropolitan Roads, I am about laying down trams along the Liverpool Road, Islington, in order that the Commissioners and the public may be satisfied of the desirableness of the system as applied to the roads of the metropolis … I have to request, therefore, that the Vestry will adjourn the consideration of Mr Train's proposals until the experiment at Islington is completed: the rails are on the ground, and within a month from this date I have reasons to believe that the line will be at work.'

Concerns were also raised by the local water and gas companies regarding the possibility of the railways causing burst pipes and that they 'may interfere very materially with the repairs, alterations and other necessary works connected with the company's mains and supply'.

Finally, the Committee's report was read out: 'The committee, having considered the application referred to them from Mr George Francis Train, dated the 9th August, for permission to lay down a street railway in the following places in this parish, recommend that the same be acceded to, and such permission be given, subject to the following conditions:

The line to be laid down from the northern boundary of the parish in the Finchley Road, along that road, the Wellington Road, Park Road, Upper Baker Street, York Place, Baker Street, east side of Portman Square, Edwards

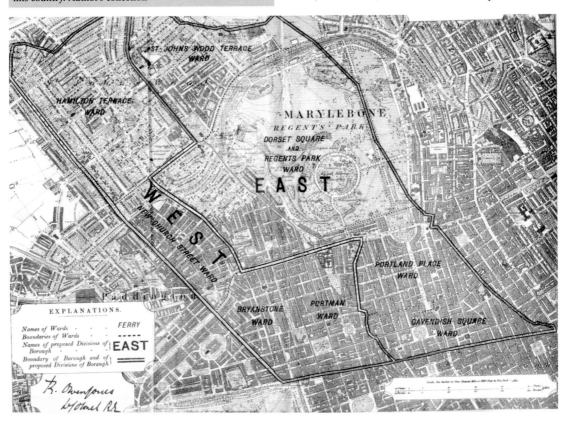

Street, Wigmore Street, north side of Cavendish Square, Cavendish Place, Regent Street, to Oxford Street, returning by Oxford Street, Portman Street, west side of Portman Square, along the line of Gloucester Place and Gloucester Street, to join the route already named in the Park Road, and a second return line to the boundary of the parish in the Finchley Road.

The whole of the works to be done at the cost of Mr Train, to the satisfaction of the surveyor to the Vestry. Mr Train to complete the works in ten weeks from the time of breaking the ground, and to have no portion of the road open for longer than a fortnight.

Mr Train, previous to the commencement of the works, to give security, satisfactory to the Vestry, to remove the rails at his own expense, and to reinstate the road in case the Vestry should at any time require him to do so.'

No decision was reached on this report as the meeting degenerated into a round of amendments and counter amendments and votes thereon. At one point someone from the floor even said that he 'presumed the real cause of the Chairman's changed opinion, in respect to this subject, arose out of his recent visit to Birkenhead, where, doubtless under the hospitable wing of Mr Train, he had been well feasted and pretty generally well cared for'. The heated meeting concluded with the passing of a resolution that: 'the whole of the proceedings be referred back to the committee further to report'.

A special Committee appointed by the Vestry to consider these matters met on Thursday 11 October 1860: 'further to report upon the application of Mr George Francis Train to construct street railways in the parish of Marylebone; also to receive and report upon applications from the London General Omnibus Company, and Mr Curtis'.

Chairman to Mr Wilkinson, the LGOC's solicitor: 'Have you any additional information to offer to the committee to that you laid before the last meeting of the Vestry?'

Wilkinson: 'I really don't know how to answer that question, for I do not know what information you require, or course of procedure you mean to adopt.'

Chairman: 'If you have any plan, such as you proposed to lay before this committee, or any improved principle of street railway to lay before us, we are ready to hear it.'

Wilkinson: 'We have yet no plan to lay before you, for

we only first heard of your approval of the scheme on or about Monday week through the public papers.'

Chairman: 'You are not prepared then to lay a plan before us at the present time?'

Wilkinson: 'Not yet. But if you will delay your decision for a fortnight, plans shall be submitted.'

Mr Curtis then stated what he proposed to do in Marylebone. He said he was going to lay down the line on the Liverpool road, which he hoped would be finished in about a month. The money required had not been deposited, as that at present was a matter to be settled between himself and his friends. He was prepared, if privilege was granted him, to lay down a similar line in Marylebone upon the same terms as the other gentlemen; and, no doubt, he could undertake to do so in a month, and at his own expense.

A 51-signature petition was then presented from the residents of Baker Street: '… It was felt by many that these proposed tramways running through such thoroughfares as Baker Street and Gloucester Place would depreciate the value of the house property at least 25 per cent. So far as Baker Street was concerned, fine shops had been opened, and they were doing all they could to convert it into a first-class business street. They were under a strong impression that if the system

STREET RAILWAYS IN LONDON.

———◆———

SPECIAL   REPORTS

OF THE

DEBATES IN THE REPRESENTATIVE COUNCIL

OF

SAINT MARYLEBONE,

UPON THE APPLICATION OF

GEORGE FRANCIS TRAIN, ESQ.,

OF BOSTON, U.S,

TO ESTABLISH

STREET RAILWAYS IN LONDON:

WITH

INTRODUCTION, INCIDENTS, OPINIONS OF THE PRESS, AND APPENDIX.

————

By Messrs. C. Greene and G. P. Rippon,

Short-hand Writers and Reporters to the London Press.

————

London:

PRINTED AND PUBLISHED BY HENRY MITCHENER, EVERSHOLT STREET, OAKLEY SQUARE, N.W.

—

1860.

The title page of the report of the 'Debates in the Representative Council of Saint Marylebone upon the application of George Francis Train, Esq., of Boston, US, to establish Street Railway in London' — the handiwork of Messrs Greene & Rippon, 'Short-hand writers and reporters to the London Press', from which these transcripts have been derived. *Author's collection*

of street railroads was adopted, such object would be wholly and entirely defeated, because the aristocracy would no doubt leave the neighbourhood, and carry the trade of Baker Street elsewhere.'

The Chairman then called upon Mr George Francis Train, to know if he had any desire to address the committee.

Train: 'I do not know that I have anything more to say; my application is before you. … I ask for no monopoly, no privileges, and will undertake all the risks, costs, and legal liabilities (if you fear any), as my only desire is to introduce in Marylebone a great improvement: a plan of street railway that has been well tried, and in extensive operation in America, and now practically demonstrated in Birkenhead, and proved to be a great blessing to those communities … I appear simply with my plans before you to lay down street railways in your parish — to extend to you a great public boon; and I will take all the risks of proving it to be so. I will assume all legal proceedings to which you may be exposed. I will reinstate the road, if shown to be a public nuisance, entirely at my own expense; it shall not cost you one shilling and I will give you all the security you like besides my rails, timber, and material on the ground. *(Cries of 'Hear, hear!')* … I have no lawyer here with me. I come among you unattended, to submit my plan in a plain, straightforward manner; and I feel assured that I know more about street railways than all the solicitors in this country. *(Laughter and applause.)* The advantages of my plan, since the inauguration in Birkenhead, are rapidly becoming known to the most of your eminent men, engineers, Members of Parliament, capitalists, as well as to the public journalists of the country, a great number of whom have got to be conversant with its practical utility. *(Applause, and cries of 'Hear, hear!')* In a short time a trial line will be in operation in Victoria Street; and if you grant my application you can have the opportunity of trying it here, as I am at any time ready to carry out my plan, I ask for no privilege, no monopoly, no favour, nor affection of any kind. I only ask you to grant me what I am willing to pay for. *(Applause.)* … I am come among you in this country with two articles of faith: first, that I am introducing to your parish a public boon; second, that my plan of street railway is the best. I leave all to you, and allow you to take whatever course you think proper. *('Hear, hear!')* I am in no hurry; take your own time to consider the matter fairly; but if you decide in my favour to-day I am ready to commence operations tomorrow.' *(Loud cries of 'Hear, hear!')*

Q: 'Allow me to ask you a question not in any spirit of opposition. Are you willing to allow any carriage to go upon your tram?'

Train: 'Certainly; but you must not have your carriage like mine. My carriage is patented, and no one can infringe upon it; and it is as much like Mr Wilkinson's plan as roast beef is to red herring, or champagne to water. I am in no opposition to Mr Wilkinson, Mr Curtis, or anybody else; the road is open to all. *('Hear, hear!')* I am quite willing for any person to use my rails; but they must not infringe upon my carriages. The experiment has been attended with the greatest success at Birkenhead, 85,000 persons having availed themselves of this boon. The fact is at that place, during the past month, more persons have travelled by my carriages than in other omnibuses for years.'

Q: 'Never mind your comparison about roast beef or red herring. I want to know this: Do you ask us to give up any part of our public roadway for your exclusive use?'

Q: 'Then, if I run a carriage with a flange upon your rail, would you proceed against me?'

Train: 'Certainly not, sir; unless it would be an infringement of my patent.'

Q: 'I have no interest at all in the matter; I simply attend here as a ratepayer, and on behalf of my fellow ratepayers, to watch over our interest; and, therefore, I wish to know if I can use a wheel with a flange to it on your rail?'

Train: 'You can if you like; but it must not be like mine. I simply ask for a trial line, and I will take it up in thirty days, or less, if required. Your question is not the right way put. I say all persons can use my rail, but they must not use my carriages.'

Q: 'It is very important to know if any wheel will run on your line of rail?'

Train: 'Yes, any wheel.'

Q: 'Then, if I have a private carriage, and choose to have a wheel to run upon the line, can I do it?'

Train: 'Any wheel would be allowed to run on the flat part of the line.'

Q: 'I want to know if permission is given to Mr Train to apply his tramway, will he do it as an experiment, and will he reinstate the road if required?'

Train: 'Yes, sir, precisely according to my application, which is before you.'

Q: 'Do you not consider that any carriage using any description of flange to run on your line will be an infringement of your patent?'

Train: 'Not at all, sir. I will take care of myself. I ask for no monopoly whatever, nor any exclusiveness; and I do everything at my own expense. My carriages do not go off the line, and have the desirable advantage of classifying the traffic, and preventing confusion. I ask for no police interference, or any other powers different to that of an ordinary individual. I feel satisfied that proper courtesy will enable me to steer clear from wilful obstruction of draymen, who, I am sure, when treated courteously, will turn out of the way; at all events I am willing to see; and, to my mind, they seem to have more courtesy than you like to give them.' *(Laughter.)*

Q: 'The law requires that travelling in this country should be under legally acknowledged rules, known to drivers as the off and nearside. Now, I want to do this. I am going across your line immediately in front of you. How am I to do it?'

Train: 'Very well, sir. I can go six miles an hour, and can pull up in less time than an ordinary omnibus. Not a single accident has happened in this way in Birkenhead since it has been running.'

Q: 'Perhaps the roads in Birkenhead are better adapted than in Marylebone?'

Train: 'No, sir; not at all. They are better adapted here than there. I think your streets are wider.'

Q: 'You are asking permission to lay down a plan, and I want to know the practical working of it. Supposing a heavy waggon of coals broke down on your tramway?'

Train: 'In reply to that question I would say: a coal carriage broke down in Birkenhead, and it was moved in two minutes and a half.' *('Hear, hear!')*

Q: 'If a wheel crowded against or got into the iron groove, would it not have difficulty to get off?'

Train: 'Not at all. There is no groove. We find no difficulty in Birkenhead.'

Q: 'Here, in the London streets, we are more crowded than at Birkenhead, and carriages run in all directions. Now, if a wheel was crowded along on the outside *(referring to Mr Train's model upon the table)*, I cannot see that it can immediately get off. How is the driver to get off? What are people to do if horses' feet come in contact with [the rails]? Is there not great danger in slipping? I ask these questions, because several people state this as a great objection to street railways, as they consider it will throw down the horses and cause great destruction to property and sacrifice of life?'

Train: 'If you will allow me, I will state what has occurred from actual experience. As regards any obstruction — of the rails, I would say they are but nine-sixteenths of an inch above the road, and so constructed that neither horses

nor carriages have suffered from the least inconvenience at Birkenhead. The improved rail is nearly flat and about five inches in width. I have not heard a single instance where the wrenching of wheels or the stumbling or slipping of horses has caused serious accident. When I opened the line at Birkenhead I took everything at my own risk. There has been, it is said, some trifling accidents; in fact, I have had bills sent in to me for £9 10s, for five accidents; and I have been advised not to take any notice of these claims by the Commissioners, as it was the results of conspiracy. *('Hear, hear!')* I would suggest, gentlemen, as I am in no hurry, and a trial line is to be tested in Victoria Street in about sixty days, that this Vestry will do nothing until they have ocular demonstration there.' *('Hear, hear!' and applause.)*

Train was then questioned by several people about accidents.

Train: 'In New York thirty-four millions of persons had travelled in one year on these lines, and only twelve met with accidents; while in New York, Boston, and Philadelphia last year the number was over seventy millions, and only fifteen accidents. In case of an accident, or necessity of any kind, the flange of his carriage wheels

A studio photographic portrait of George Francis Train, taken while he was in the UK promoting street railways. His frozen stare probably comes from the fact that the exposure time on such photographs was anything up to two minutes — a long time to stand still for someone of Train's energy! *Author's collection*

'Victoria', one of G. F. Train's 'carriages' as depicted in the frontispiece illustration to his pamphlet 'Observations on Street Railways', which was addressed to the Rt Hon Milner Gibson MP, President of the Board of Trade. The carriage has 'BAYSWATER' on its side and 'SHEPHERDS BUSH' and 'NOTTING HILL' on its roof. The illustration was pure fantasy — when it did open, Train's Bayswater line did not reach Marble Arch, although the carriage is possibly quite an accurate depiction. *Author's collection*

were so simply arranged by a double tread that the carriage could at any time leave the rails; but he did not wish to adopt this plan of leaving the rails as a rule, because immediately the public knew he could get off, it would be fatal to the system. He contemplated the introduction of his scheme would have the desirable advantage of classifying the traffic, remove the present confusion; and that every carriage of his would displace three omnibuses.'

Q: 'What is the reason you have not got it down in your Broadway, New York?'

Train: Simply, sir, because there has been so many applicants that a difficulty has been raised as to who should have it. For instance, like on the present occasion of my application, Mr Curtis's, and the London General Omnibus Company's. *(Laughter, and cries of 'Hear, hear!')* But it will be laid down in Broadway next year.'

Q: 'What is that thoroughfare in comparison with the traffic of many of the streets of this city?'

Train: 'Why, it is the Cheapside and Ludgate Hill of Philadelphia and the traffic is equal to those streets in proportion to the population.'

Q: 'To what extent do you suppose the traffic is lessened in New York by these street railways?'

Train: 'It would have required 1,000 more omnibuses than at present in New York to have conveyed the people who used these carriages last year.'

Q: 'I would ask the gentleman — if he got permission of this Vestry without an Act of Parliament, would he have the exclusive right over and above everybody else?'

Train: 'Yes, because my carriage is patented.'

Q: 'Is that the case in America?'

Train: 'There is no patent on the carriages in America; but the right of road is still preserved, and we have been working seven years without interference. Immediately another carriage meets mine it has to go off, because the public understand my carriage cannot move off, and it preserves the line of route. This is allowed by general consent.'

Q: 'If this scheme of yours was adopted in Cheapside and Ludgate Hill, what amount of traffic do I understand you to say it would dispose of?'

Train: 'Why, one of my carriages will displace three omnibuses!'

The specially appointed committee then reported that 'the committee met, and elicited from the solicitor of the London General Omnibus Company, that they would not be prepared with any plans to submit for a fortnight, and Mr Curtis stated that he would not be in a position to lay his plans fully before them for a month. Mr Train, however, was prepared with the plans he had previously submitted, and also expressed his willingness at once to enter into bonds to lay down his tramways within a given time, and to take them up again at his own expense, upon notice by the Vestry that they desired them to be discontinued. The committee saw no necessity for delay, and, therefore, again recommended that Mr Train's plan be adopted, and his offer accepted.' It was resolved that a decision be made upon the plans next Saturday.

On Friday 19 October 1860 a special meeting in opposition to street railways was held at which 80 people were present. All spoke against Train's proposals and street railways in general. The result was a resolution which expressed the meeting's 'earnest protest against any such scheme, believing the adoption of which would most seriously injure the interests of the inhabitants, and impede the general traffic of the road'.

In total 10 deputations, nine memorials and 11 letters were read out against Train's proposal, mainly citing its assumed detrimental effect upon property prices and loss of privacy. The lively and at times riotous meeting ended with the adoption of the following amendment: 'That, having regard to the representations made by inhabitants on the line of thoroughfare, and as no Act of Parliament has yet been obtained to authorise or make regulations respecting street railways in the metropolis, it is not advisable at the present time to grant Mr Train's application to lay down street railways in this parish.'

A fourth meeting was therefore convened on Saturday 27 October 1860. To simplify matters, Train withdrew his amended application laid before the second Vestry meeting, '… in order that the question under the consideration of the Vestry may not be complicated unduly. All he is anxious to do is to lay down the originally proposed experimental line, feeling sure that when this has been done the rest will be seen to be a public necessity.'

Several ratepayers' memorials were then presented against the proposal. Four new communications received since the last meeting were also read out — all referred to financial loss or damage to property. There were then two deputations, following which Train was again invited to address the meeting:

Train: 'This system of street railways is not an experiment, as you must believe, when I inform you there are no less than 600 miles in operation in the streets of various towns and cities in America. It is either a good thing or a bad thing — either a great truth or a great lie. *(Loud cries of 'Hear, hear!')* I have always heard, and long believed, that a part of the British Constitution was fair play, and not to condemn any system without a fair hearing and a fair trial. *(General applause.)* All I ask, then, is simply this — that I may come into the great parish of Marylebone, and demonstrate to you the principle at my own expense; and, if it is an injury, it will only be so for four weeks' time, for

> Also featured on the frontispiece of Train's pamphlet was 'Napoleon III'. Showing 'PADDINGTON' on its side, this double-deck carriage is a double fantasy in that Train's Bayswater line did not reach Paddington and double-deck vehicles were not used. Access to the upper deck appears to be via a ladder, as the chap in the light-coloured top hat is demonstrating. It all looks more than a tad precarious! *Author's collection*

'THE PEOPLE' worked G. F. Train's second demonstration line in London, which ran along Victoria Street and opened on 15 April 1861. Victoria Street runs east–west from Victoria station to Broad Sanctuary at Westminster Abbey; it was constructed in the 1850s and required the demolition of many slum houses. Victoria station had opened on 1 October 1860, just six months before Train's line was laid. This is the only known photograph of any of Train's London 'experiments'. The majority of the street has been redeveloped. *Author's collection*

I place money in your hands to take it up again. In one month, if it is disapproved of, I will have the whole of the tramway removed, and the streets restored to their original state … With regard to the deputations and their petitions, I would state that at Birkenhead, where my first experiment in England has been carried out, a few persons in Grange Lane and other localities petitioned against me, and afterwards some of those parties sent in memorials in my favour. *('Hear!')* Although the street railway there has only been in existence seven weeks, it has carried 85,000 passengers. As to the gentlemen from Portman Square and Portland Place, I will at once relieve them of their fears, by withdrawing my application, so far as they are concerned, although I feel assured that these game gentlemen will do as they did at Birkenhead, petition in favour of it, when they see my plan in operation — for it will be in London very shortly. *(Much applause.)* All I now desire is that you will give me a trial in any street that does not interfere with the lordly mansions of Portman Square. If this meeting will give me permission, I will confine my present operations to Oxford Street, from the Marble Arch to Tottenham Court Road, and I will place ample security in gold in your hands, with the portrait of the Queen stamped upon it, if you think that sufficient, for the

faithful performance of my contract, for taking the whole of the line up again, if disapproved of, within four weeks. *(Loud cries of 'Hear, hear!')* I sincerely thank you, gentlemen, for your courtesy in listening to me, which is what I have always heard of an English audience. *(Applause.)*

Q: 'Do I understand you will indemnify the parish against all actions and all risks that may be brought against the Vestry by reason of your laying down and carrying out the works necessary for laying down the railway, and take it up again at your own cost, within four weeks, if disapproved of?'

Train: 'Certainly. I consider it is all a one-sided bargain in your favour. I am perfectly willing to take upon me all risks, all liabilities, and all legal proceedings of whatsoever kind.' *('Hear, hear!')*

Q: [Did Mr Train] 'expect to have his experiment in Victoria Street speedily opened?'

Train: 'I do, but, as there would probably be but very little traffic there, comparatively, I think that might be used as an argument against my plan, and therefore I am desirous of bringing the railway before their own doors, so that they might see and judge of it, where there really was traffic. I might mention a point I had omitted, which was, that the Vestry of Lambeth had appointed a special committee to go down to Birkenhead, and on their return he had no doubt but that they would report in favour to the Vestry, to permit him to lay down a line through the Clapham Road.'

Q: 'If the Board allow Mr Train to lay down his tramway, would he object to other omnibuses or vehicles of the same gauge running over it?'

Train: 'My carriages were patented, and he should have no apprehension of any others running over the line — it would be open for all.'

Q: 'Will you indemnify any tradesman for loss to his business by your railway?' (Cries of 'Oh, oh!' and laughter.)

Train: 'Certainly, my carriage is patented; but so far as the line is concerned it is open to all, although made at my expense. I have been before the vestry of Shoreditch, and their committee have reported in favour of my being permitted to lay a line through Shoreditch, where there is as much traffic, or nearly so, as in Oxford Street.'

Q: 'Have you applied to the parish of Kensington?'

Train: 'Yes; and they could not grant permission, as the streets there are principally under the control of the commissioners of metropolitan roads.'

Q: 'I believe Fifth Avenue, New York, is inhabited by a similar class of persons to those residing in Portman Square, and also that there is no line of street-railway in Fifth Avenue.'

Train: 'That is the case, as there were at the outset so many applications. They could not, therefore, obtain the charter till last year; but in last year's session of the Legislature the charter [the Gridiron Bill] was granted for

The menu and loyal toast from the Yankee Breakfast hosted by G. F. Train at the Westminster Palace Hotel to launch his Victoria Street line on 15 April 1861. The meal was based on that served 'à la chemin de fer Americaine' (sic). Beneath the 'Toast to Victoria Queen of Empire' Train reported the 'Latest Police Intelligence — Marylebone Police Court, Hope v, Train'. It reads: 'Mr Yardley decides that assent of Commissioners of Road is a License [sic] — that the rail is not an obstruction, but that rule of road is infringed on account of there being but a Single Line. Fine, One shilling — Informer's profit, Sixpence. Driver of Furniture Van fined 10/- for obstructing Street Rail Car, with recommendation to be more particular another time.'

Fifth Avenue, and for forty-eight additional streets in New York.' *('Hear, hear!')*

Q: 'I believe also that you have not permitted one to be laid down in the Broadway?'

Train: 'For the same reason there is not one yet laid down in the Broadway; but the charter was passed for that in the last session of the Legislature.' *('Hear, hear!)*

As the debate raged and time went on, during a vote Train sent the Chairman the following note:

'Sir —

Observing the opposition, and not wishing to cavil in antagonism with so large a parish — a stranger to all of you — I hereby desire that you will postpone all action upon this matter until you can see the system underway in Victoria Street.

I am, Gentlemen, your obedient Servant,

George Francis Train'

As soon as the Chairman had subdued the uproar that again ensued, he put the resolution to adjourn the question for three months, which was carried with six dissentients. The Board, after a lengthened debate of between six and seven hours, then adjourned, in great excitement.

The debate was widely reported in both the national and local press. The *City Press*, in its edition of 2 November 1860, probably best summed it up: 'Friend Train has applied the brake and brought himself to a stop, for fear of a collision. The hungry Omnibus Company tried to eat him up, but he was too large a mouthful; so the old enemy and the old friend of change, public opinion, hoisted a signal, and brought him to a pause. "There is a tide in the affairs of men," and Mr Train's tide is yet to come, and by him, or some other bold spirit, omnibus tramways will yet be carried out. While we are waiting for the fever to subside in Marylebone, and the experimental line to grow into practical shape, let us consider whether there is any other means of escape from the fever and the fret of creeping cabs and immobile omnibuses.'

There was also much correspondence from outside London, both in support of and against Train. This example is possibly an example of both, but also indicative of the attitude of the times. From 'a friend in Cheshire', dated 5 November 1860: 'Would you like to know the reason why you are not taken notice of by the most respectable people of Liverpool, Birkenhead ... and your cleverness in setting up a Street Railway (which in itself is an excellent invention and public benefit) not appreciated? Well, it is because you are sinning against God your Maker, by directly breaking one of His holy commandments, and desecrating His holy Sabbath-day by causing these carriages to run on Sunday — adding to England's national sin of Sabbath-breaking, and putting a temptation in the way of the lower classes that they would not otherwise have.'

George Francis Train emerges well from all of this. He comes over as intelligent, persuasive; wily even. It is curious to speculate that the furore aroused by his application to the Marylebone Vestry may have set the London authorities so against ever having trams penetrate the heart of the capital. After all, horses were an everyday sight in the streets, as were carriages, so was it just the rails that were at issue? If such a comparatively minor innovation could stir up such emotion, it is therefore perhaps less difficult to appreciate how, a couple of generations later, the spectre of trams powered by a 'phantasmagoria' like electricity was so opposed.

Train himself was 'bloodied but unbowed' by his experiences at Marylebone, and in 1861 he both laid and ran three demonstration lines in the city:

23 March 1861	Porchester Terrace–Edgware Road (closed September 1861)
15 April 1861	Victoria Street (closed 6 March 1862)
15 August 1861	Westminster Bridge–Kennington Gate (closed 21 June 1862)

Collectively, depending upon how long into September 1861 the first line was operational, Train gave Londoners between 797 and 827 days' experience of tram travel, in the process carrying over 2,000,000 people and taking around £20,000 in fares — a very able demonstration indeed!

2. '…the great revolution in tramway fares …'

The London United Tramways

Two generations after George Francis Train's demonstration lines, it would again be private enterprise that brought London its first proper experience of electric tramways. Upon the formation of the London Passenger Transport Board, with effect from 1 July 1933, tramways built by private companies contributed 29% of the total route mileage and 20% of the combined car fleet. These were the results of the cumulative enterprise of three companies — the London United Tramways Ltd, the Metropolitan Electric Tramways Ltd and the South Metropolitan Electric Tramways & Lighting Co Ltd. Since 14 June 1913 all three had been under the control of the London & Suburban Traction Co Ltd, which had been formed by the British Electric Traction Co and the London Underground Railways Group on 20 November 1912. After 1933 the former company lines bore the brunt of the route closures and car withdrawals, an unceremonious end for systems that were once the epitome of modernity. Something of their former glory and importance, plus a good measure of the investment they represented, remains in the accounts published at or around the time of their opening.

The London United Tramways (LUT) had the distinction of bringing electric trams to the streets of London. The company was formed on 19 July 1894, to acquire the assets of the West Metropolitan Tramways Co Ltd, which had gone into receivership. The latter had built up a small network of horse tramlines from Shepherd's Bush to Kew Bridge and Hammersmith. When the West Metropolitan's assets were finally acquired in August 1894, the LUT's General Manager, James Clifton Robinson, set about making the company work. He scrapped the older one-horse cars and put the staff into uniforms. Gradually the company returned to profitability, but Robinson's real ambition was to electrify the tramways using the overhead trolley system, and to expand the network. To these ends Robinson used his charisma and persuasive powers to gain the support of most of the local authorities and committees through whose areas his projected lines passed but met with resistance to overhead wires from the LCC. To bypass this Robinson planned lines which were mostly outside LCC jurisdiction. A Bill for the electrification and extension of

SIR CLIFTON ROBINSON.

Sir James Clifton Robinson (31 December 1848 – 6 November 1910), the General Manager of London United Tramways. He was born in Birkenhead and, at the age of 12, saw G. F. Train's first tram run there and later became acquainted with him. *Ian Allan Library*

the LUT's tramways was placed before Parliament in 1898, but some of the proposed lines were removed in the Parliamentary process, and it was a trimmed and amended Bill that became law on 2 August 1898.

Construction work on the LUT's first electric line started in Brentford on 20 March 1899 and was substantially completed by June 1900, but the opening was delayed by objections over electrical insulation from Greenwich and Kew observatories. These also embraced those underground railways which were embarking upon electrification at the same time, and the situation was deemed sufficiently serious for a conference of all interested parties to be held in October 1899, which attracted much public and trade press interest.

The first technical details of the system

The first technical details of the company's system were published in the trade press in October 1899 'through the courtesy of Mr J. Clifton Robinson, managing director of the company. Some 27 miles are being run by horses, and on the electrical section both the overhead trolley and the conduit systems will be used … The trolley portion of the system will cover about 20 miles, and is now under construction. It is on that part of the route which is nearest London. The line will be run on the three-wire system, and two trolley wires will be carried over each track, making a complete metallic return. The two inside wires will be inter-connected, and will form the neutral pole of the system. The overhead wires will be divided into half-mile sections, and, in order to meet Board of Trade requirements, each 1½ miles of the line will be supplied by an independent feeder running direct to the power station. The neutral return will also be reinforced for each section of a mile and a half by a separate feeder. The conduit system will have cast-iron yokes every 5ft and a concrete sub-structure. Hand-holes will be placed every 15ft and manholes about every 150ft.

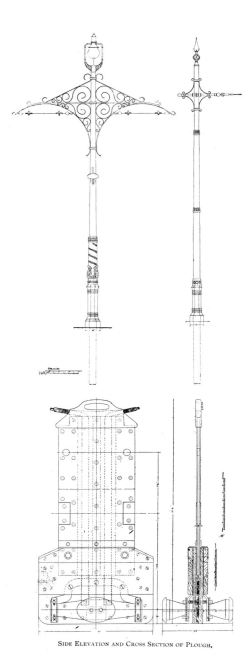

So determined was James Robinson to see the LUT electrified that he accommodated all interests in his proposals; these included a 1½-mile section of line between Hammersmith and Young's Corner which would operate on the LCC's conduit system, which the latter had just adopted but not yet built any lines using it. These are the details of the conduit, plough and traction poles which the LUT announced in October 1899. *Ian Allan Library*

The slots will be ¾in in width and the conductors will be T irons, held in porcelain insulators. The plough will provide a sliding contact by means of shoes held against the contact rails by spring pressure. The cars will be double-decked, mounted on maximum traction trucks, and … are of very pleasant design.

They will be 33ft 4in overall, the length of the body outside being 21ft 11½in, and the length of the body inside 21ft 4in. The width of the car at belt rails will be 6ft 6in, and the height from the track to the top of the roof when the car is empty, 9ft 9½in. From the track to the top of the trolley standard the height will be 15ft 2in. The cars will have cross-seats on the top and longitudinal seats inside.'

'… undaunted pluck and indomitable perseverance …'

Work on constructing the LUT's first section of electric tramway proceeded apace; this included the power station, repair shops and car sheds at Chiswick. However, the whole enterprise was thrown in doubt by seemingly innocuous demands from authorities connected with the Greenwich and Kew Observatories. They alleged that if the LUT's rails were used as the current return, stray or leaked currents would injuriously affect the readings on certain instruments used to measure variations in the earth's magnetic field. Although these were no more than 'hypothetical', a series of meetings, which began in October 1899, failed to bring about any resolution of the matter over the course of a year, by which time the LUT's

SIDE ELEVATION AND CROSS SECTION OF PLOUGH.

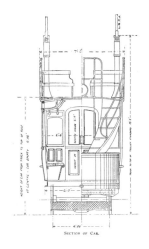
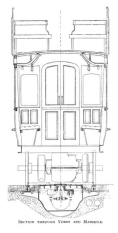

SECTION OF CAR.   SECTION THROUGH YOKES AND MANHOLE.

Cross-sections of the first LUT cars. The one on the left shows that they were to be equipped with twin trolley poles, which were thought to be an unavoidable necessity to overcome the objections from Greenwich Observatory. One of the cars was exhibited at the International Tramways & Light Railways Exhibition at the Royal Agricultural Hall, which opened on 22 June 1900. The livery was scarlet and white. *Ian Allan Library*

first section of tramway was completed. Therefore, over half a million pounds' worth of the company's capital lay idle and continued to do so for another six months, whilst horse trams worked the new lines beneath dead electric wires.

The *impasse* was broken by George White — the LUT Chairman — through a direct appeal to HM Treasury. The solution? To '… remove the delicate instruments from Kew to some place beyond the radius of the supposed malign influence'. An agreement to this effect was signed at the Treasury on 3 April 1901, under which the latter agreed to pay £10,000 for the removal of the Kew Observatory to Eskdalemuir, in Dumfriesshire. Within an hour of this '… preparations for acting on this arrangement were taken'.

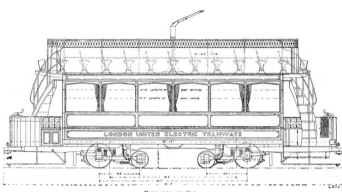

ELEVATION OF CAR.

The LUT's ambition for its electric tramway extended to its cars, which, it hoped, would be sufficiently elegant to obviate the need for people to hire private carriages. This is the elevation of one of the first 100 cars ordered from Hurst Nelson. The curtains at the lower-saloon windows hint at the luxury afforded. *Ian Allan Library*

The opening and formal opening

So, finally, the LUT could open and at 7.00am on the morning of 4 April 1901 7½ miles of electric tramway route — the first in London — were brought into operation. Three lines were opened that day:

Shepherd's Bush–Acton (2 miles 5 furlongs)
Shepherd's Bush–Chiswick–Kew Bridge (3 miles 6 furlongs)
Hammersmith–Young's Corner, Chiswick (1 mile 1 furlong)

That morning 'the entire working of the system was changed. Horses and horse-cars disappeared from the West London tramways, and 100 elegantly appointed electric tramway carriages have from that day been running frequently at one-minute intervals for some 20 hours a day without interruption and without mishap. At times the pressure of traffic has been phenomenal. On Good Friday, Easter Day, and Easter Monday the cars were not only crowded within and without, but vast crowds struggled for a place at the various termini, so much so that the company had to requisition its construction gangs from the extension lines to preserve order and protect the cars from being swamped. On Whit Monday, although the immediate novelty has worn off, the pressure was even more severe than before. Splendid weather prevailed, the full complement of rolling stock was kept on the lines, and a record was established for 7 miles of tramway such as had never been attained in this country. It may be stated that on Sunday, Monday, and Tuesday of Easter week, the cars conveyed 385,000 passengers, while for Whit Sunday,

'Ealing's Double Event' — a cartoon commemorating the inauguration of the LUT, the incorporation of the Borough — the first municipal one in Middlesex — and also the building of 'workmen's dwellings', the latter being facilitated by new legislation. James Robinson is depicted on the top deck of car No 101, acknowledging the crowds. *Author's collection*

"A Double Event"

Whit Monday and Tuesday the record increased to 443,000 passengers, the maximum in one day being reached on Whit Monday, when the passengers numbered 210,657 or an average of 2,100 people conveyed on each car.'

The system was not formally opened until 10 July 1901, jointly with the next three extensions:

Acton–Ealing–Hanwell (2 miles 7 furlongs)
Hanwell–Southall (2 miles)
Kew Bridge–Brentford–Hounslow (3 miles 1 furlong)

Adding eight route miles to the system, these more than doubled its length. Then in session in Parliament was a further Bill, which would, if authorised, see the system expanded to 80 route miles.

Reports of the formal opening noted that it '… will enable the company to bring before the public eye — and the public purse! — more effectually than has ever yet been done the great revolution in tramway fares which the introduction of efficient electric traction has brought about.'

Some 420 guests were invited to the formal opening and Lord Rothschild performed the honours. The party was conveyed 'from the terminus at Shepherd's Bush over the route to Southall and thence to Chiswick, where the visitors were entertained to luncheon'. In his speech, Lord Rothschild congratulated the LUT for 'having chosen a populous district for their undertaking, avoiding those sylvan glens and monastic institutions which they had decided to keep intact'.

The LUT had its headquarters in High Road, Chiswick. 'Within their property, covering an area of four acres, the company have erected their model power

station. The depot is shaped like the letter Y, with the narrow end to High Road, and at the left-hand side of the entrance the attention of the visitor is at once attracted by the pleasing architectural features of the long range of administrative offices, within which rooms are provided for the managing director and engineer and his staff, the board room, the offices for the traffic superintendent of the line, the inspecting staff, reading rooms and other accommodation for the outdoor staff and apartments for all the various subordinate departments of the administration. Beyond these, and facing the entrance, are the commodious car sheds.'

The central power house

'This handsome building, measuring 154ft in frontage, has a total depth of 106ft, divided internally into two main portions — the engine room and boiler room. The internal walls of both of these divisions are faced with glazed bricks, and the engine room floor is laid with mosaic tiles. It is a model power house in all respects.'

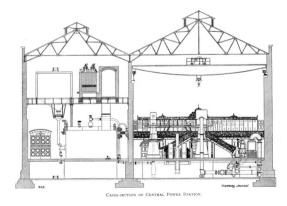

CROSS-SECTION OF CENTRAL POWER STATION.

The boiler room

The boiler room at Chiswick was 'state-of-the-art' and relied upon electrically powered equipment. 'The boiler room, which occupies the back portion of the building, consists mainly of a steel-frame structure, designed to carry the heavy weights of the coal-storage bunkers (which contain 500 tons of coal), the flue, the economiser, and the feed-water tanks, all of which are located on a floor above the boilers. ... The equipment consists of ten horizontal water-tube boilers, each capable of evaporating 11,000lb of water per hour at a steam pressure of 150lb per sq in ... The total heating surface in each boiler is 3,140sq ft. Arranged in five batteries of two boilers each, the boilers [are fed] by a mechanical stoker ... [from overhead bunkers, themselves fed by a mechanical bucket chain] capable of handling 40 tons of coal per hour, and driven electrically by a 10hp motor.' The boiler feed water was pumped by steam and drawn from a softening plant capable of treating 10,000 gallons per hour, having first been drawn from one of three wells by an electric pump.

The engine room

'The engine room is 60ft wide and a 25-ton electric overhead travelling-crane traverses its length of 154ft. ... There are ... two vertical cross-compound condensing engines with cylinders 22in and 44in by 42in stroke, running at 90 revolutions per minute, with a steam pressure of 150lb at the throttle. Each of these engines is directly connected to two 250kW compound-wound continuous-current (DC) generators, one placed on each

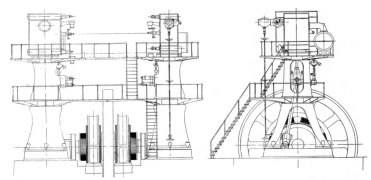

The LUT's Chiswick power station initially contained two vertical cross-compound condensing steam engines, directly connected to two 250kW compound-wound continuous-current (DC) generators, one on each side of the flywheel, the arrangement of which is seen in these side and end views from August 1901. *Ian Allan Library*

side of the flywheel. ... The variation in speed does not exceed 2½ per-cent from no load to full load. These engine sets are used for supplying current to the lines in the vicinity of the power station, and in addition there is now one 500kW ... three-phase set for the transmission of power (AC) to the sub-stations. The latter run at 90 revolutions per minute, and to each is directly coupled a 5,000V 32-pole three-phase alternator, the frequency being 25 cycles per second.'

A photograph of the engine room, which is of the same date as the previous drawings, shows the cleanliness of the building and the elaboration of the decoration used — note the floor tiles around the machinery. *Ian Allan Library*

Glimpsed in the previous photograph at the far end of the engine room was the switchboard, seen here in more detail. Its gallery was 9ft above floor level and reached by the decorative symmetrical staircases. The 27 panels on the board were formed from white marble! *Ian Allan Library*

The switchboard

Power was distributed via a switchboard which was 'erected at the south end of the engine room, upon an ornamental gallery 9ft from the floor level. It consists of white marble panels 7ft 6in high by 2ft wide, bolted to angle-iron frames, there being twenty-seven panels in all. The board extends practically the whole width of the room, one half being for the continuous-current panels and the other for the three-phase panels. The continuous-current board consists of four railway generator panels, two booster panels, eight feeder panels, one Board of Trade panel and one instrument panel. The high-tension board contains three three-phase generator panels and eight three-phase feeder panels. The switches and bus bars for the high-tension current are supported by joists in a closed chamber underneath the switchboard floor, the switches being of the oil-break type, and operated through levers on the switchboard.'

The car-sheds and machine shop

Completing the extensive facilities at Chiswick were extensive car sheds '... capable of accommodating 100

A block plan of LUT's central power station, car sheds and repair shops at Chiswick. This emphasises the scale of investment that developing such a tramway represented for the company. *Ian Allan Library*

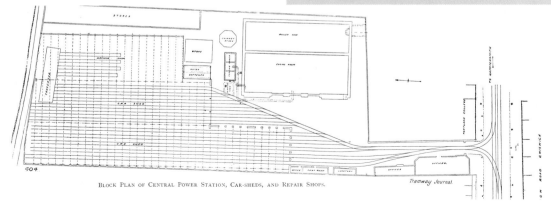

BLOCK PLAN OF CENTRAL POWER STATION, CAR-SHEDS, AND REPAIR SHOPS.

Tramway Journal

electric cars, and a complete series of repairing shops. ... The sheds, which contain eleven lines of track in all, are furnished with pits for inspection purposes, and all the movements of the cars to, from and within the sheds and shops are effected electrically by the trolley wires. The machine shop is provided with wood-working plant and machine tools for car repairs ... . With these machines all repairs to car bodies can be effected. ... The north end of the structure is devoted to the repair of the motors and car trucks ... . A large amount of space is here allotted to benches fitted with vices, etc. At the north end is an electric traverser, working over the tracks in the shop and over three tracks in the running shed.'

Rolling stock

Standing idle for six months had been the LUT's fleet of 100 new tramcars 'specially designed for this system. Each car is mounted upon two four-wheeled bogie trucks and is equipped with two 25hp electro-motors, weighing 1,480lb each, and each capable of exerting a horizontal effort of 1,270lb on a 30in car-wheel at a speed of 8mph. There are seats for 69 passengers — 30 inside and 39 outside. ... The cars have been designed and constructed with every regard for the comfort and convenience of the travelling public. Handsomely fitted and luxuriously upholstered internally, they afford an

admirable illustration of the most advanced form of public conveyance, while the seating outside consists of reversible benches designed in the most comfortable shape, and elegantly fitted in coloured woods.'

Concluding the speeches at the formal opening on 10 July 1901, James Clifton Robinson provided a living link to London's first tramway venture by recalling '... another inauguration 40 years ago at which I was present as the most humble member of staff — when George Francis Train opened, at a function such as this, the small first development of tramways in Europe'. Concluding his thanks, he also included '... the eight million Londoners who, since our tentative opening thirteen weeks ago, have patronised and popularised our electric cars'. Noting too glances from the company Chairman to sit down, Robinson closed with: 'It is an old chestnut, but it may lighten our feelings, as I beg to appreciate the point, if I ask: "Why was George White?" Because, possibly, "Robinson Crusoe".'

In reporting the opening *The Light Railway & Tramway Journal* declared that the LUT had '... by undaunted pluck and indomitable perseverance brought their undertaking to a pitch of perfection which excites the admiration even of those who are avowed opponents of tramways of any description whatever'.

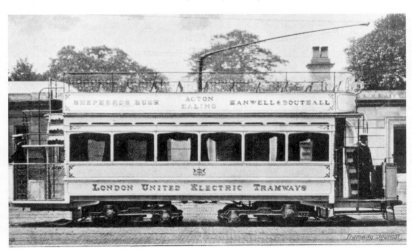

From this point the LUT developed just over 53 miles of electric tramways, mostly in the west of London, between 1901 and 1907:

13 August 1903	Hounslow–Hounslow Heath and Isleworth–Twickenham
8 November 1902	Hampton Court via Hampton Wick
4 April 1903	Hampton Court via Hampton
1 June 1904	Uxbridge
1 March 1906	Hampton Wick–Surbiton and Surbiton–Tolworth
26 May 1906	Brentford–Hanwell and Kingston Hill–Malden
27 April 1907	Malden–Raynes Park
2 May 1907	Raynes Park–Wimbledon Broadway
27 June 1907	Wimbledon Hill Road–Merton and Haydon's Road–The Plough

At the end of July 1915 the LUT opened its last extension, of its Acton terminus, by 159yd, to join up with lines of the Metropolitan Electric Tramways (MET), by which time the company had lost its independence within the London & Suburban Traction Co Ltd.

Tangible reminders at Chiswick

Coaches of British European Airways had been using Chiswick tram depot since at least 1947 to operate the bus service between Heathrow Airport and the West London Air Terminal in Kensington. In 1978 it was refurbished as a bus garage in a £2 million scheme and reopened as Stamford Brook in 1980. The garage closed in 1996 and became a store for unlicensed vehicles for possible future use. It reopened in 1999 and was operated by London United Busways, who, in a tangible link with its history, operated buses branded as 'London United'. However, between April and September 2006, the company commenced to rebrand all of its vehicles with the Transdev name and logo.

The largest and most visible remnant of the LUT is the former Power House in Chiswick, designed by William Curtis Green and J. Clifton Robinson and now a listed building. The two large female figures that grace its façade represent 'electricity' and 'locomotion'. Although largely superseded by Lots Road (Chelsea) power station from 1917, the Chiswick installation remained in use as Goldhawk substation until the closure of the trolleybus service in 1962. The 260ft-high chimney was demolished in 1966, but the building was preserved by London Transport in 1976 and has now been converted into flats.

One former LUT car also survived. The lower saloon of Type W car No 159 was discovered at Ewhurst Green, Surrey in 1978 where, together with two others, it had been used as living accommodation. It was recovered and put into storage in Derbyshire before undergoing full restoration at the National Tramway Museum at Crich.

Shepherd's Bush Tube station and tramway terminus seen in the early days of LUT operation of its new system in July 1901 with two cars in view, the one on the right being No 53. On the left is a stockpile of setts, indicating that not everything was finished at the opening! *Barry Cross collection / Online Transport Archive*

A pair of LUT cars seen outside the company's headquarters at 74 High Road, Chiswick. *Barry Cross collection / Online Transport Archive*

LUT cars Nos 4 and 182 at Brentford Bridge in the early 1900s, with what appears to be a contractors' compound to the left and a third car pulling up behind No 4 and otherwise the road pretty much to themselves. No 182 became London Transport No 2524. *Barry Cross collection / Online Transport Archive*

Uxbridge terminus with car No 15, crew and an inspector, probably at or close to the opening of the line there on 1 June 1904. This postcard view was probably coloured — note the marked absence of overhead wires above the tramcar! The covered wagon plying up the hill (far right) is an impressive sight too. *Barry Cross collection / Online Transport Archive*

Did 'A. G.' run out of space on the back of this postcard? Anyway, the recipient can have been left in no doubt of the level of approbation accorded the new LUT service: 'You will find this a very pleasant trip to Uxbridge'. The car is No 87. To the left a gaggle of telegram boys are in an excited huddle! *Barry Cross collection / Online Transport Archive*

THE LONDON UNITED TRAMWAYS, LIMITED.

Route No.	Route.	Journey Times, Intervals, Fares.
7	**Uxbridge & Shepherds Bush** Via Uxbridge Road, Hillingdon, Hayes, Southall, Hanwell, Ealing, Acton.	Time 68 mins. Interval : Wkdays 12 mins. Sundays 8 mins. Fare 1/-
7a	**Southall & Shepherds Bush** Via same roads as Route 7 between these points.	Time 37 mins. Interval : Wkdays 6 mins. Sundays 6 mins. Fare 7d.
7c	**Hanwell & Shepherds Bush** Via same roads as Route 7 between these points.	Time 27 mins. Interval : Wkdays 6 min. Sundays 4 mins. Fare 6d.
55	**Hanwell & Brentford** Via Boston Road.	Time 13 mins. Interval : Wkdays 8 mins. Sundays 10 mins. Fare 2d.
57	**Hounslow & Shepherds Bush** Via High Street Hounslow, London Road Isleworth, High Street Brentford, Kew Bridge, Chiswick High Road, Goldhawk Road.	Time 40 mins. Interval : Wkdays 10 mins. Sundays 10 mins. Fare 7d.
63	**Kew Bridge & Shepherds Bush** Via same roads as Route 57 between these points. Extended to Brentford during week-day rush hours.	Time 19 mins. Interval : Wkdays 10 mins. Sundays 10 mins. Fare 3d. Time 24 mins. Interval 8 mins. Fare 4d.
67	**Hampton Court & Hammersmith** Via Hampton Court Road, Church Street, Hampton High Street, Hampton Hill, Wellington Road, Hampton Road, Twickenham Green, King St., London Road, Twickenham Road, High Street Brentford, Chiswick High Road, King Street Hammersmith.	Time, 61 mins. Interval : Wkdays 8 mins. Sundays 10 mins. Fare 10d.
69	**Twickenham & Kingston** Via Hampton Road, Stanley Road, Broad Street, High Street Teddington, Kingston Road, Hampton Wick, Kingston Bridge.	Time 28 mins. Interval : Weekdays 6 mins. Sundays 10 mins. Fare 6d.

THE LONDON UNITED TRAMWAYS, LIMITED—continued.

Route No.	Route.	Journey Times, Intervals, Fares.
71	**Hampton Court & Wimbledon** Via Hampton Court Road, Kingston Bridge, Clarence Street, Cambridge Road, Kingston Road, New Malden, West Barnes Lane, Raynes Park, Worple Road. (Additional Cars work between West Barnes Lane and Wimbledon during week-day rush hours.)	Time 44 mins. Interval : Wkdays 6 mins. Sundays 9 mins. Fare 6d. Time 14 mins. Interval : Wkdays 6 mins. Fare 2d.
73	**Kingston Hill & The Dittons** Via London Road, Eden Street Kingston, Penrhyn Road, Claremont Road, Victoria Road, Brighton Road, Portsmouth Road.	Time 26 mins. Interval : Wkdays 10 mins. Sundays 15 mins. Fare 3d.
77	**Tolworth & Richmond Park Gates** Via Ewell Road, Victoria Road, Claremont Road, Penrhyn Road, Eden Street Kingston, Richmond Rd., King's Road. (Additional Cars work between Kingston (Eden Street) and Tolworth during week-day evening rush hours.) (Additional Cars work between Surbiton Station and Kingston Eden Street on Saturday afternoon and evening only.)	Time 27 mins. Interval : Wkdays 10 mins. Sundays 15 mins. Fare 3d. Time 22 mins. Interval : Wkdays 10 mins. Fare 2d. Time 10 mins. Interval : Sat. afternoons & evenings 12 mins. Fare 1d.
81	**Summerstown & Haydons Rd. Junct.** Via Plough Lane, Haydons Road.	Time 8 mins. Interval : Wkdays 20 mins. Sundays 20 mins. Fare 1½d.
89	**Acton & Hammersmith** Via Acton Vale, Askew Road, Paddenswick Road, King Street Hammersmith. Part Service extended to Hanwell on Saturday afternoons and evenings	Time 19 mins. Interval : Wkdays 4 mins. Sundays 5 mins. Fare 3d. Time 34 mins. Interval 8 mins. Fare 6d.
2 4	**Wimbledon Hill & Victoria Embankment** Via Merton Road, Tooting Broadway, Balham High Road, Clapham Road, Kennington Gate, Westminster Bridge. **Hampton Court & Victoria Embankment** Extension of the above routes via same roads as Route 71 on Saturday afternoons and on Sundays from May to mid-October only.	Time 58 mins. Interval : Wkdays 3 mins. Fare 6d. Time 99 mins. Interval : Sat. aft. 12 mins. Sundays 8 mins. Fare 11d.

An LUT timetable for 1928, showing the routes, service intervals and fares in operation at that time. *Author's collection*

Above: On 16 May 1931 the LUT introduced the first trolleybus service in London using vehicles based on AEC chassis with bodywork by the Union Construction & Finance Co of Feltham. The first to arrive were Nos 4 and 5, depicted here on inaugural-day 'Special' workings in a contemporary advertisement placed in the trade press by the chassis builder. *Author's collection*

Above right: Three former LUT tram routes formed the basis of the first tram-to-trolleybus conversion undertaken by London Transport. This was on 27 October 1935 and is summarised in this block which formed the basis of both advertisements and flyers issued by LT. *Author's collection*

Right: Ex-LUT car No 159 undergoing restoration at the National Tramway Museum at Crich. This was state of progress on 19 September 2009. The car's characteristic straight stairs are in place, as is a solitary upper-deck seat. *Author*

On and from October 27, Trolleybuses will be substituted for trams on routes as shown below:

Tram Route		Trolleybus Route
ROUTE	SECTION BETWEEN	
26	Hammersmith and Kew Bridge	667 — Hammersmith and Hampton Court — every 3 minutes to Kew Bridge — every 6 minutes to Hampton Court
67	Hammersmith and Hampton Court	
57	Shepherds Bush and Hounslow *The Bell*	657 — Shepherds Bush and Hounslow (Wellington Road) — every 4 minutes
63	Shepherds Bush and Kew Bridge	

Certain early and late journeys between Young's Corner and Hammersmith Broadway now operated by route 26 will not be continued by the Trolleybuses.

TIMES of first and last Trolleybuses are shown overleaf.

3. '… one of the most fertile fields in the entire world for electric traction'

The Metropolitan Electric Tramways

Of the tramways absorbed into the London Passenger Transport Board on 1 July 1933, the former Metropolitan Electric Tramways Ltd's (MET) contribution to both the route mileage and the tramway fleet was second only to that from the LCC Tramways. By then one of three tramway undertakings controlled by the London & Suburban Traction Co Ltd, the MET was also the largest constituent concern, forming 56% of the Group's route mileage and 61% of its tramcar fleet.

The MET's first line — Wood Green–Harringay–Finsbury Park — opened on 22 July 1904, but even before this, the tramway world was fair agog with expectation. A full three months before the first line opened the MET was described as '… one of the most promising and important offspring of the British Electric Traction Co' and that '… it is hardly too much to say that the company will very shortly serve one of the most fertile fields in the entire world for electric traction'.

A lot had been achieved in 10 years. The company was registered as the Metropolitan Tramways & Omnibus Co Ltd on 21 November 1894, adopting its more familiar name on 13 January 1902. A deal of the attention that the company attracted was in no small measure due to the celebrity of its chairman — Emile Garcke. He was born in Saxony, Germany in 1856 and came to England when he was very young, becoming a naturalised British subject in 1880. As a young man he joined the Anglo-Brush Electric Light Corporation Ltd, an American subsidiary, as Secretary in 1883, rising to become Manager in 1887 and Managing Director of its successor company, Brush Electrical Engineering Co Ltd, four years later. In 1893 he also joined the Board of a reconstructed Electric Construction Co Ltd, based in Bushbury, Wolverhampton. There Emile Garcke was responsible for the reconstruction of the commercial side of the business, which had failed in July 1893.

Always a strong supporter of electric traction, with the help of fellow directors from his various interests, Garcke set up the British Electric Traction Co Ltd (BET) in 1896, becoming its Managing Director. By 1904 the BET was a vast group of 66 companies, mostly associated with tramways and distribution supply. Emile Garcke was the mastermind behind the enterprise, which by 1906 operated 15% of all British tramways. Throughout his life he was also a keen publisher of books and pamphlets on electrical topics, and in 1887 wrote, jointly with John Fells, a pioneering work called *Factory Accounts, their Principles and Practice — A Handbook for Accountants*. This set out the principles of cost accounting for those working in manufacturing businesses and has remained in print. He also instituted the *Manual of Electrical Undertakings*, which was first published in October 1896. This edition listed just 200 undertakings, but by the time of his death it had grown to a veritable 'brick' of a book, just over 2,000 pages long and commonly known as 'Garcke'. Of whatever value these manuals were at the time of publication, they have become a resource of inestimable worth to historians. Howsoever his business interests changed, Emile Garcke remained Chairman of the MET until his death on 14 November 1930, at the age of 76.

Thus, wherever Garcke went, the press followed, and developments in all of his interests were keenly followed. He was also a very vocal opponent of municipal trading, particularly with regard to electricity generation and tramway operation: 'In the case of gas, water and tramway undertakings, local authorities have (ownership of public rights of way) in perpetuity; these rights are granted to private capitalists for specific terms and unless the private capitalist is very much encouraged and has facilities offered to him, instead of obstacles put in his way, he is very much hampered to supply the commodities and render these public services on anything like the favourable terms that a municipal corporation could do.' As a result of this celebrity, his opponents called Garcke 'Oligarcke'.

Preparatory work for the MET's operation began in July 1903 when, via BET, the company acquired 43,652 £1 ordinary shares and 1,710 £10 shares in the North Metropolitan Electric Power Supply Co, which held perpetual rights to supply bulk electricity to substantial parts of Middlesex, Hertfordshire and Essex. In the light of Emile Garcke's interests and beliefs, this acquisition is entirely understandable. Later, on 24 February 1904, Garcke announced that the North Metropolitan Tramways Co (established by Act of Parliament on 12 July 1869) '… has sold or is on the point of selling, all its tramways outside the London County Council area. It has sold its lines in Middlesex to this company. … The Harrow Road & Paddington Co owns 2¾ miles of tramway which are being operated by horses, but at a tenure until 1907. Last year it obtained an Act of Parliament which authorised the conversion of the line to electric traction and we have made an agreement with that company to purchase the entire undertaking upon terms to be agreed. … If all goes well, this company will be operating in the course of the ensuing summer several miles of tramways and light railways on the overhead system of electrical traction.'

Giving further details of the business agreements made, Emile Garcke said: 'We have to share surplus profits with the County Councils. In the case of the Middlesex light railways we receive 4½% on our capital and the Council receive 4½% on their capital, and the surplus profits … are divided as to 45% to the Council and 55% to the company. In the case of the Hertford Light Railway, the Council received 4% on their capital and we received 6% and the surplus … is divided as to 40% to the Council and 60% to the company. The lease of the lines will be until 1930 in the case of Middlesex and in the case of Hertfordshire 42 years from the date of confirmation of the Light Railway Orders.'

The MET's scheme was for a mostly double-track system using the overhead method of current distribution. The company stated clearly that it had '… no desire to emulate the costly conduit experiments of the London County Council'. Indeed, the respective county surveyors and engineers in the counties of Hertfordshire and Middlesex constructed the track on behalf of the company!

The main power station was to be at Brimsdown, near Ponders End, and from it — and a newly acquired station at Willesden (bought from the Council for £72,034) — current would be distributed at 10kV to substations at Edmonton, Wood Green, Chipping Barnet, Finchley and Hendon. The main car sheds and repair works were to be at Hendon, but in the meantime existing depots at Edmonton, Manor House and Wood Green were being retained. The latter was to serve initially as the main car shed. It could accommodate 62 cars on seven tracks over pits and had a permanent-way yard.

A new chief car building and repair-shop facilities were proposed for Hendon, where 8½ acres of land had been purchased for the purpose. This would accommodate a 16-road depot, each with pits beneath, housed within four adjoining car sheds. The roads were reached via a depot fan. Initially the depot would accommodate 32 cars but its ultimate capacity was designed for 128.

Power for the system was to be generated mostly by a new power station at Brimsdown, on the banks of the River Lea, at a point north east of Enfield and Ponder's End. This would supply all but the north-western section of the tramways, which would draw its power from the company's newly acquired Willesden station.

The Brimsdown power station would be served by both canal, for bringing in coal and other materials and for the disposal of ash, and rail, once a siding had been constructed from the adjacent Great Eastern Railway. Its six boilers would each evaporate 15,000lb of water an hour, this steam being used to drive three Parsons turbines of 1,000kW output each which, in turn, drove three Brown-Boveri generators which rotated at 1,500 revolutions per minute and produced three-phase, 50-cycle electricity at 10,000 volts. This was stepped down to 550 volts DC at each of four sub-stations at the depots in Edmonton, Wood Green, Finchley and Hendon. Brimsdown Power Station was designed by the architect C. W. Grey and erected from designs by G. Hooghwinkel, the Brush Electrical Engineering Co being the general contractor for the work. A distinctive feature of the site was the 125ft chimney, which, despite its final brick cladding, was actually built from steel and supplied by Piggott & Co.

Of the company's initial 20 miles of route, horses were working 8½ miles and 11½ were light railways under construction. Special trackwork was being supplied by Hadfields of Sheffield and the tracks were to be paved by hard or soft wood block, except on gradients where granite setts would be used.

A feature of the MET's system was the use of centre poles for long sections of its routes in Tottenham and Finchley, where road widths permitted, these being of a particular design which included arc lamps for street lighting purposes.

Elsewhere side poles and span wires were used, the latter especially at Tottenham and Wood Green, where the narrowness of the streets required the use of rosettes attached to buildings. The MET was particularly set against the use of bracket arms.

Rolling stock had been ordered (unsurprisingly) from the Brush Co, and this was for an initial 150 double-deck cars of two kinds — Class A (which were larger) and Class B. There was also some variation between cars of the same class with regard to their seating, some being in rattan, some in bent wood and others having cushions.

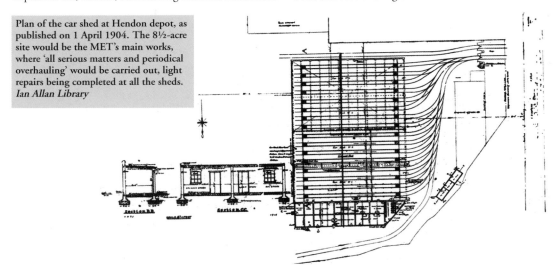

Plan of the car shed at Hendon depot, as published on 1 April 1904. The 8½-acre site would be the MET's main works, where 'all serious matters and periodical overhauling' would be carried out, light repairs being completed at all the sheds. *Ian Allan Library*

Precisely dated photographs are rare, so this view of the con-struction work on the MET's Brimsdown Power Station, situated on the banks of the River Lea northeast of Enfield and Ponder's End, dated to 13 January 1904, is a valuable record. The river can be seen curving around the site on far right. *Ian Allan Library*

Opening and progress

The company's first electric line — between Wood Green, Harringay and Finsbury Park — opened on 22 July 1904, and was followed by 40 more lines up to and including Ponders End–Enfield, the company's last, on 20 February 1911.

The Light Railway & Tramway Journal for 3 September 1909 contained a major review of tramway developments in London to that date. For the MET the news was mixed. Route mileage was 52.5, almost at the maximum the company ever attained and in the previous year extensions had been opened in Enfield, Acton, Willesden, Friern Barnet, Hendon and Finchley; 50 new cars had also been purchased, but the repair works at Hendon, although 'being built' were 'not yet completed'. Its operating figures for 1908 were as follows:

The most striking feature of the Brimsdown site was the 125ft-high chimney. It was also unusual in being of steel construction, the product of Piggott & Co of London and Birmingham. This view was recorded from across the Lea; boats bearing construction materials can be seen in the foreground. *Ian Allan Library*

Traffic receipts	£300,012
	(up £55,812 on 1907)
Surplus	£52,317
Passengers carried	57,369,307
Car miles run	6,361,253
Average receipts per mile	11.32d
Average receipt per passenger	1.25d

A further report on 'Progress to date' appeared in *The Light Railway & Tramway Journal* for 4 March 1910, which included a map of the system (see page 32):

Like the LUT, on 1 January 1913 control of the MET passed to the London & Suburban Traction Co. When the MET was taken over by the London Passenger Transport Board on 1 July 1933, it operated 53.51 miles (86km) of route. The company owned 9.38 miles (15km) of track, with the remainder being leased from Middlesex or Hertfordshire County Councils. The company owned 316 tramcars.

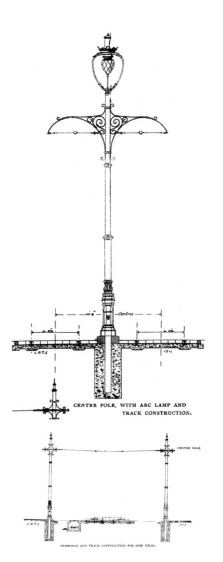

CENTRE POLE, WITH ARC LAMP AND TRACK CONSTRUCTION.

CENTRE POLE.

OVERHEAD AND TRACK CONSTRUCTION FOR SIDE POLES.

Left: A distinctive feature of the MET's system was its use of centre poles situated in between pairs of running lines. An example is illustrated here. The design is very elaborate and decorative, incorporating an arc lamp for street and track lighting. Foundations for the track consisted of a 6in-thick concrete bed. The contractors for the work were Messrs Dick, Kerr & Co Ltd. *Ian Allan Library*

Below left: On narrower sections of the MET system, such as in Tottenham and Finchley, side poles and span wires were used, as illustrated here. Note the camber of the roadway and the duct to the left, which was for the feeder cable and other necessary services. Reached via hatchways, the ducts obviated the need to dig up a lot of the road to effect repairs. *Ian Allan Library*

Below: A view of Seven Sisters Road early in 1904, before the MET's electric tramways opened. Track and overhead construction seems to be almost complete, although the little heap of material by the kerb indicates that there were still a few things to be done. The road, which nowadays forms part of the A503, was authorised in 1829 and constructed by the Metropolitan Turnpike Trust in 1833. *Ian Allan Library*

Left: Another section of the MET equipped with side poles, span wires and lamp standards. Note the horse tram in the distance (centre right); also that the traction pole to the left of the barrel-laden cart has still to be painted! *Ian Allan Library*

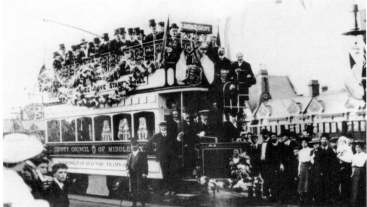

Below left: MET A-Type car No 81 seen on the opening day of the system — 22 July 1904. The car is laden with flags and swags, besides being top-heavy with top-hatted dignitaries. The destination blind shows 'BRUCE GROVE', which is in Harringay. *Barry Cross collection / Online Transport Archive*

Below: Another opening-day scene, with MET A-Type car No 77 (later London Transport No 2412) being pursued by a motor car. The locals have really gone to town on the decorations — every traction pole seems to be swathed, and flags abound. This gives a very good impression of the innovation in people's lives which the coming of an electric tramway represented. *Barry Cross collection / Online Transport Archive*

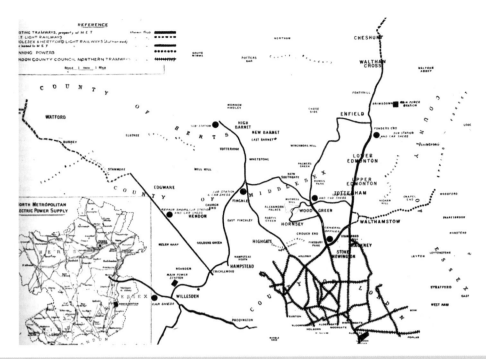

REFERENCE

EXISTING TRAMWAYS, property of M E T .... shown thus
.....T LIGHT RAILWAYS
...DDLESEX & HERTFORD LIGHT RAILWAYS (Authorised)
... leased to M E T
...NNING POWERS
...NDON COUNTY COUNCIL NORTHERN TRAMWAYS

Above: A map showing the MET system in early 1910; the inset map (bottom left) shows the district served by the North Metropolitan Electric Power Supply Co, which was a wholly owned subsidiary of the company. *Ian Allan Library*

Below: On 3 December 1904 the MET opened a separate section from Cricklewood to Edgware via Hendon. Seen here, probably on the opening day, is 'A'-type car No 106, with 'CRICKLEWOOD' on its destination blind and some form of decoration on its upper deck. The car did not survive into London Transport days, being written off after overturning at Colindale. *Barry Cross collection / Online Transport Archive*

Above: Possibly another opening-day scene — the 'SPECIAL CAR' destination is the giveaway — with MET 'A'-type car No 100, which became London Transport No 2458. There is an air of informality about this photograph, which makes it much more like a snapshot than the somewhat staid and posed views typically seen on such occasions. *Barry Cross collection / Online Transport Archive*

Right: A scene at Highgate Arch, with MET 'A'-type car No 112 (later London Transport No 2437). The Arch carries Hornsey Lane and also marked the boundary between the counties of London and Middlesex. This was also a junction between the LCC's conduit system and the MET's overhead wires; No 112 has its trolley boom down, and the conduit slot can be seen moving towards the left-hand running rail. *Barry Cross collection / Online Transport Archive*

Right: Apart from one motor car parked at the kerb, a fairly empty MET 'A'-type car, No 97 (later London Transport No 2429), is the only powered vehicle on the streets of Willesden. The scene is full of period detail, especially the hanging sign proclaiming 'This is KNIGHT'S AS ADVERTISED. The LARGEST BOOT REPAIRERS in The WORLD.' — quite a claim! *Barry Cross collection / Online Transport Archive*

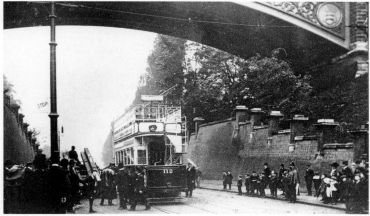

On a sunny day MET 'A'-type car No 101 (later London Transport No 2430) waits at Barnet terminus before departing for Highgate; in the background is the Church of St John the Baptist, which was extensively rebuilt in 1875. The church stands at the junction of the two roads which unite to form the High Street; locally, the top of its spire is claimed to be the highest point between there and the Ural Mountains, some 2,000 miles to the east! *Barry Cross collection / Online Transport Archive*

Busy times at Golders Green! Met A-Type car No 75 (later London Transport No 2416) will easily load to capacity here. Given the dress of the passengers, this is possibly a Sunday short working of what became MET route 40, which ran between Cricklewood and North Finchley only up to 2.30pm each day. *Barry Cross collection / Online Transport Archive*

MET No 214 (later London Transport No 2258), a Type F car of 1908, working what would become MET route 29 (Enfield–Euston). The five cars of this class were the first the company bought ready-fitted with top covers. *Ian Allan Library*

A pair of MET cars working on the conduit: 'A'-type No 73 (later London Transport No 2415) and 'T' No 307 (later London Transport No 2357) pass in traffic during the 1920s, the former's progress being impeded by a bus which has just swung out in its path. *Barry Cross collection / Online Transport Archive*

Guide to MET tramway services in 1928, listing the 23 routes it was operating at that time. *Author's collection*

Ex-MET 'H'-type car No 82 became No 2253 in London Transport's fleet, being seen here working route 19 (Barnet–Euston) on the overhead-wire section north of Highgate. The dates on the side poster for the Commercial Motor Transport Exhibition at Olympia reveal that this photograph was taken in 1935. All cars of this type would be withdrawn by January 1939. *D. W. K. Jones / Ian Allan Library*

4. A 'sudden' tramway to Sutton
The South Metropolitan Electric Tramways & Lighting Co Ltd

One of the most distinctive tramway undertakings in London was the South Metropolitan Electric Tramways & Lighting Co Ltd, known as the 'SouthMET'. Although a small undertaking, the SouthMET was larger than all of the local authority tramways bar West Ham and constituted just under 4% of the tramways absorbed into the LPTB in 1933. The company was registered as the County of Surrey Electrical Power Distribution Co Ltd on 19 April 1899 and its name was changed to the now more familiar one on 7 August 1904. The company's electricity supply undertaking commenced its public supply in March 1902 and from 12 December 1915 they began taking bulk electricity supply from the County of London Electricity Supply Co. Ltd. The Home Counties Joint Electricity Authority acquired the concern with effect from 1 July 1932.

The SouthMET was an offshoot of the British Electric Traction Co, from which it acquired the powers and rights to build three tramway lines: Croydon RDC's Light Railway Order for Mitcham & District, which comprised powers to build 3¼ miles of double-track route the powers under the Croydon & District Electric Tramways Act, 1902, to build 11.2 miles of tramwaythe Croydon & District (Extensions) Act, 1903, to build 4.35 miles.

It also entered an agreement with Croydon Corporation for mutual running powers between Crystal Palace and West Croydon station. Given its location, the SouthMET had high hopes: 'The company's system, as a whole, ought to yield excellent results, seeing that much of it passes through well-populated areas, and in other parts will serve districts which are undergoing rapid development on a large scale.' Indeed, BET saw this as but a start to a larger network of south London lines, based on Croydon, through the construction of connecting lines to schemes already authorised. Ultimately, not all of this materialised, and, along the way, the company had to overcome a number of obstacles, including a large amount of road building.

The SouthMET's lines and aspirations are encapsulated on a map published in December 1906.

The company received its first Board of Trade certificate on 13 February 1906, and, by the date of the accompanying map, the company had opened the following lines:

A 'Country Section' of the SouthMET, with two cars (a second one is in the far distance, moving towards the camera) in a photograph illustrating the opening of the full system in December 1906. This very rural aspect emphasises the amount of construction that this relatively modest tramway system required. Note the tree planting on either side of the road. *Barry Cross collection / Online Transport Archive*

Pawleyne Arms–Thicket Road	12 April 1906
Robin Hood–Low Level Station	12 April 1906
Croydon–Tooting	26 May 1906
Penge	1 June 1906
Croydon–Sutton (part)	10 November 1906
Croydon–Sutton (whole)	21 December 1906

For most of the tramway the centre was Croydon, 'where the terminus of the company's system is in Church Street, not far from the West Croydon Station of the London, Brighton & South Coast Railway. The section between Croydon and Mitcham Common, via Tooting, is about 5¼ miles in length. After leaving the centre of Croydon, this line passes through a populous working-class quarter, and Mitcham (where the population is

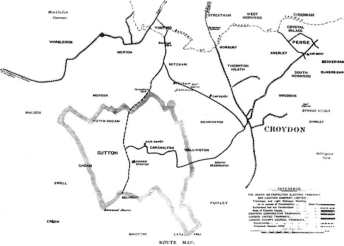

ROUTE MAP.

The first tram in Ruskin Road, Carshalton on 27 October 1906, alongside Carshalton Park. A paper label declares this to be a 'PRIVATE CAR', and it seems to be replete with company officials and surrounded by local children — it was a Saturday, so they weren't at school! This section of the route, as far as the Windsor Castle Inn on Carshalton Road, opened on 10 November 1906. *Barry Cross collection / Online Transport Archive*

increasing rapidly), to the boundary of the County of London at Tooting. There it will afford connection with the authorised lines of the London United Tramways Co., as well as with the London County Council Tramways when their extensions have been constructed. By means of this line, therefore, when all is completed, there will be tramway intercommunication between Croydon, Mitcham, and all parts of London.'

The system map also showed about 2¾ miles of line 'which is completely detached from the other sections, namely, that which serves parts of Anerley, Penge, Beckenham, South Norwood and the Crystal Palace. This section is not yet completely constructed, but the principal portion of it has been in operation for several months past, and is of great utility as giving passengers from the Croydon Tramways access to the Crystal Palace.'

Small though the company's system may have been, at 13 miles, 1 furlong and 5 chains, the SouthMET nonetheless saw itself as playing a strategic role in extending journeys by tram all across London and beyond: 'In the course of time it will be possible to ride by tramway from Sutton or Croydon in the extreme south of the Metropolitan area, to Barnet or Enfield in the north, Hampton Court or Kingston in the west, and to West Ham or Ilford in the east, all of which represent journeys of considerable length and duration.'

The years 1905 and 1906 saw near-frenetic activity for the SouthMET, most of its lines being constructed at this time. A lot of the work went into a number of road improvements, especially in the Carshalton area, where the company also built a number of new roads, which, it declared, constituted '… an improvement of the highest local importance and value, which has been effected without the ratepayers having to find a penny of the cost'.

On 13 February 1906 the SouthMET received its first certificate from the Board of Trade that a portion of the tramways was fit for public traffic. One of its lines — that between Croydon and Sutton via Waddon and Wallington — was built with such haste that the trade press dubbed it the 'Sudden Tramway'. The reason for the haste is unclear, but it may have been due to the imminent lapsing of powers acquired from BET; under the terms of a tramway Act, powers to construct lines and operate a tramway lasted for five years.

By contrast, the junction of Anerley Road and Croydon Road, photographed at the same time as the previous shot, presents an altogether more urban aspect. To the left is the Robin Hood Inn, on the corner of Croydon Road and Oak Grove Road (later Elmers End Road) — a very steep hill. The SouthMET's Penge depot was on Croydon Road, just to the left of the pub, which burned down in 2006. *Barry Cross collection / Online Transport Archive*

The scene at the junction of Tamworth Road with Lower Church Street, Croydon, recorded in a photograph published in December 1906 to illustrate its overhead work. Lower Church Street led to Mitcham Road, which is where the car shown centre left is bound. The Eagle Inn was then tied to the Forest Hill Brewery, which was established in November 1885 and operated it until taken over by Whitbread in 1924. *Ian Allan Library*

Given the time constraint, 'This was no slight task to perform, especially in view of the heavy amount of road widening which had to be carried out concurrently with the laying of the track. It was duly accomplished, however, the ten miles of track and all the improvements being carried out in six weeks. The rails were rolled by 20 June (1906) and the first car was run on 8 August, the Board of Trade inspection following on 11 August. The first car had to be drawn from Croydon on a lorry, with horses as the motive power. ... All the work on this section ... was done by the Brush Electrical Engineering Co Ltd, with the exception of the paving, which was done by William Griffiths & Co Ltd. The material ... consisted, in the Borough of Croydon, of creosoted wood blocks 4in deep, laid on a floated concrete bed, with a granite edging composed of one course of setts supplied from Guernsey quarries, 6in deep by 4in wide, laid at the outside of the wood block margins. A portion of the track in the borough and all the track in the Urban District Area of Sutton is laid with specially dressed Norwegian setts, 5in wide by 4in deep, which form a very smooth surfaced road. ... The rest of the track is paved with Norway granite setts of the ordinary 4in by 5in type, and in this work a very rapid rate of progress was maintained, some 18,000sq yd of track being paved in five weeks — a performance which speaks well for the resources of this firm [William Griffiths & Co Ltd].'

From the dates given above it seems that all this activity was sufficient for at least part of the Croydon–Sutton line to pass a Board of Trade inspection, and the company's powers thereby be retained, although it is known that the track in Stafford Road, Croydon, was found not to be up to standard — hence the delay in the opening of the route to public working.

The SouthMET's rolling stock comprised 51 cars, 41 of which were mounted on four-wheel trucks, the remainder being bogie cars. The former cars seated 26 passengers on top and 24 inside, the bogie cars seating 30 and 28; the body colour was green.

Again, for such a small system the SouthMET was well endowed with depots. 'The system possesses three car depots; the principal one at Carshalton [incomplete in December 1906] is of double span with iron and steel framing [then being built by Dick, Kerr & Co Ltd]. ... it will accommodate 60 cars, and will also have repairing and painting shops. ... There are separate pits under the tracks, and the platforms between, as well as the floor of the repair shops, are concreted.

This will constitute the principal depot of the company, and will be entered from the road through an ornamental brick portal. The Penge and Croydon car sheds are brick-built with galvanised iron roofs, and were built, respectively, by Dick, Kerr & Co Ltd and W. Taylor & Co, Hammersmith. These two sheds have accommodation for 26 cars. ... At Penge there are repair shops, as this portion of the system is quite isolated from the other sections and therefore must have its own facilities. All the depots have the usual offices and conveniences, stores, etc, and all have the front end open, without doors or shutters.'

On the commencement of its tramway service the SouthMET purchased current from local authorities but was also in the course of erecting its own power station at Sutton, 'where two turbo-generators of 250kW each by C. A. Parsons & Co are being installed. To make room for these an extension of the buildings has been made.' The power station was working by 1908, when, it was noted, despite this, '... most of the current is purchased from Croydon at 2d per unit ... or from Beckenham or Penge'. That year was also the first full one that the completed system operated. It produced the following statistics:

Miles opened	
Route miles	13.09
Single line	0.19
Double line	12.90
Number of passengers carried	6,911,094
Average receipt per passenger	1.45d
Number of cars in stock	51
Traffic receipts	£41,884
Total traction receipts	£42,408
Balance, gross receipts (trams)	£16,667
Balance, gross receipts (power)	£3,982
Electricity sold (BTU)	604,007

SouthMET car No 36 in Church Street, Croydon. It's an autumn day, and smartly turned-out children pose with a few adults and tram crew — possibly a school or Sunday School outing on the new tramway. *Ian Allan Library*

When published on 7 December 1906 this series of photographs was captioned 'Views on the System' — they are more than that! The date is 8 August 1906 and the location is Sutton. Car No 25, one of 10 owned by BET, used by Croydon Corporation and transferred to the SouthMET, was drawn there on a lorry by horses. The second and third images show the body being raised on jacks, while fourth shows the truck being manoeuvred into position. Job done, the remaining shots show the car being driven under power. On 11 August the line passed its Board of Trade inspection. *Ian Allan Library*

Car No 25 again, seen here in Stafford Road, on the Sutton line, in August 1906. Again the destination blind is showing 'SPECIAL CAR', indicating that this was part of the car's delivery run on loan to the Corporation, as described previously. Note how the trolley boom is working at quite an angle to the car; also the workmen to the left, who appear to have stood down from their task to let the car pass. *Barry Cross collection / Online Transport Archive*

The SouthMET's Penge car shed, offices and gates were built by Messrs Dick, Kerr & Co and could accommodate 26 cars. Here they are seen when new and complete. The single-track access was off Croydon Road and curved sharply left before entering the depot past the offices. To the right, surplus land is being offered to let or lease. *Ian Allan Library*

The SouthMET's Croydon depot was in Aurelia Road, off Mitcham Road, and was built by W. Taylor & Co of Hammersmith. Like Penge, it accommodated 26 cars. The central two roads were also equipped with pits, as seen here. To the left is a line of the BET cars loaned to the Corporation; these were numbered 36-45 in the latter's fleet but became Nos 17-26 in the SouthMET fleet. *Ian Allan Library*

The front of the SouthMET's Sutton depot, which was off Westmead Road, Carshalton, and in an incomplete state when photographed in November 1906. Built again by Dick, Kerr & Co, its twin sheds accommodated 60 cars and the site also had repair and paint shops. Access to the depot, which was situated well back from Westmead Road, was via an ornamental brick portal. *Ian Allan Library*

Mitcham Common, Croydon.

The SouthMET's days of 'independence' were brief. Control of the SouthMET was transferred to the London & Suburban Traction Co Ltd with effect from 14 June 1913. As with all other tramway undertakings in London, control of the SouthMET was vested in the London Passenger Transport Board (LPTB) with effect from 1 July 1933. The Board immediately sought savings in their operation, and those tramways which had worn track and which operated older types of car were an obvious target. The SouthMET suffered as a result of this, and its routes were closed within four years:

6 December 1933	West Croydon–Penge route abandoned and converted to bus operation
8 December 1935	Croydon–Sutton line converted to trolleybus operation
9 February 1936	Croydon–Crystal Palace line converted to trolleybus operation
12 September 1937	Croydon–Tooting–Willesden line converted to trolleybus operation

The closure of the Croydon–Crystal Palace line also deprived Londoners of the opportunity to ride on the top deck of an open-top double-deck tramcar.

Two of the SouthMET's three depots also closed at the same time, the third surviving to the present day. Croydon became better known as Mitcham depot and was disused after 1926. It was used briefly in 1936 for the breaking up of cars displaced by trolleybuses. Penge depot was closed with the end of its tram services on 8 February 1936; its cars were broken up on site. Carshalton depot was converted for trolleybus operation from 1935 (and for motor buses from 1959) and closed on 29 January 1964. It still stands and is now in use as a self-storage warehouse.

Fair Green, Mitcham.

The SouthMET's Mitcham-route terminus was at Fair Green, where car No 17 — ex Corporation No 36 — was photographed. There is a wealth of detail here, including the 'Little Wonder' coffee house to the left and the splendid clock-cum-weather vane-cum lamp to the right. This was of the sewer-venting kind, running off 'surplus' methane! *Barry Cross collection / Online Transport Archive*

An unidentified SouthMET car approaching the terminus at Tooting Junction, with the destination blind already changed to 'CROYDON'. Tooting Junction station is to the left, and the posters behind the tram and curving around the bridge parapet (right) provide fascinating detail. *Barry Cross collection / Online Transport Archive*

The view in the opposite direction at the same location, with Tooting Junction railway station on the right and SouthMET car No 20 (ex Corporation No 39) pulling up behind a second car. Among the posters facing the station is one for the annual Horse Show at Olympia. *Barry Cross collection / Online Transport Archive*

The first of two views of car No 37 recorded on 30 May 1918 in Stanley Park Road at its junction with Woodcote Road, Wallington, on the SouthMET's Sutton route, this being by the Town Hall and Library. The conductor ushers passengers into the lower saloon, whilst a man with a walking stick crosses behind the car. *Barry Cross collection / Online Transport Archive*

On the same occasion four passengers wait their turn to board No 37 as a woman on the upper deck looks down. The car has been fitted with its 'Spencer hoop' — a loop of steel above the top of each staircase, designed to protect passengers from being struck by the trolley boom as it moved down low when the cars passed beneath low bridges. These were fitted at about this time and were named after Christopher Spencer, General Manager of the London & Suburban Traction Co's combined tramways. *Barry Cross collection / Online Transport Archive*

SouthMET cars Nos 15 and 2 in Tamworth Road, Croydon, with a Corporation car in the 1920s.
Barry Cross collection / Online Transport Archive

In 1930 SouthMET cars Nos 1-16 were reconditioned. The work included fitting transverse seats in the lower saloon, which was also rebuilt from three windows to four. New controllers were also fitted, as were LCC-style route boards, all seen here on car No 3 at West Croydon.
Barry Cross collection / Online Transport Archive

THE SOUTH METROPOLITAN ELECTRIC TRAMWAYS AND LIGHTING CO., LTD.

Route No.	Route.	Journey Times, Intervals, Fares.
4	**Penge & West Croydon** Via Beckenham Road, Croydon Road, Penge Road, Norwood Junction, Selhurst Road, Northcote Road, Whitehorse Road.	Time 30 mins. Interval : Wkdays 9 mins. Sundays 9 mins. Fare 4d.
5	**Crystal Palace & West Croydon** Via Anerley Road, Penge Road, Norwood Junction, Selhurst Road, Northcote Road, Whitehorse Road.	Time 29 mins. Interval : Wkdays 9 mins. Sundays 9 mins. Fare 4d.
6	**Mitcham (Fair Green) & West Croydon** Via Mitcham Common, Croydon Road, Mitcham Road, Tamworth Road.	Time 30 mins. Interval : Wkdays 9 mins. Sundays 9 mins. Fare 5d.
7	**Sutton & West Croydon** Via Benhill Avenue, Carshalton Road, Ruskin Road, Park Road, Stafford Road, Epsom Road, Waddon Old Road, Tamworth Road.	Time 32 mins. Interval : Wkdays 6 mins. Sundays 7 mins. Fare 6d.
8	**Mitcham (Cricket Green) & Victoria** Via Fair Green, Mitcham Road, Tooting Broadway, Balham High Road, Balham Hill, Clapham Road, South Lambeth Road, Vauxhall Bridge Road.	Time 46 mins. Interval : Wkdays 4 mins. Sundays 6 mins. Fare 7d.

PLACES OF INTEREST ON THE SYSTEM.

	Route No.
Banstead Downs	7
Beddington Park and Old Church	7
Croydon Empire	4, 5, 6, 7
Crystal Palace	4, 5
Duppas Hill	7
Grand Theatre, Croydon	4, 5, 6, 7
Mitcham Common (Prince's and Tooting Bec Golf Links)	6
Mitcham Green (one of the oldest Cricket Grounds in England)	6
Penge Empire	4
Waddon Aerodrome	7

INFORMATION FOR PASSENGERS.

WORKMEN'S TICKETS. On the L.U.T., M.E.T. and S.M.E.T. Systems Return Tickets for Workmen are issued on all Cars completing journeys before 8.0 a.m., the charge being the ordinary single fare, with a minimum of 2d. Return journeys may be made at any time the same day, but only between the fare points travelled on forward journey, as indicated by punch hole in the ticket.

CHILDREN'S TICKETS. On all three Tramway Systems children under 3 years of age are carried free unless occupying seats. They must be accompanied by paying passengers. Children from the age of 3 and under 14 years are carried at reduced fares with a maximum of 1d. For further particulars see Fare Bills in Cars.

THROUGH SINGLE JOURNEY TICKETS WITH "UNDERGROUND." Through Tickets are issued from the London United Tramways to certain Stations on the Underground System in the West End, West-Central Districts and the City, via the following Exchange Stations :—

CHISWICK PARK	Routes .. 57, 65, 67
EALING COMMON	" .. 7, 7a, 7c
HAMMERSMITH	" .. 67, 89
SHEPHERDS BUSH	" .. 7, 7a, 7c, 57, 65

Similar facilities are in operation between the Metropolitan Electric Tramways and Stations in the North-West and West-Central Districts and the City, via the following Exchange Station :—

GOLDERS GREEN	Routes 40, 60

Information as to Fares can be obtained from the Companies' Servants, or from the Bills exhibited in the Cars. In most cases there is a saving on a Through Ticket.

TIME TABLES of the various services are exhibited at important points en route. For times of first and last cars the Conductor should be consulted.

ALTERATIONS. Due notice of alterations which may be made to services shown herein will be given by Bills exhibited in the cars and en route.

LUGGAGE. On all three Tramway Systems personal luggage, workmen's tools and children's folding mail carts are carried free of charge.

2d. per package is charged for all merchandise, empty crates and similar articles carried on the platform.

Articles will only be carried if accompanied by a passenger, at owner's risk and at the discretion of the Conductor.

Conductors are instructed not to allow any package to be taken inside or on top of the car or left on the rear platform if it is likely to cause inconvenience to other passengers or impede the Conductor in his duty.

INFORMATION FOR PASSENGERS—contd.

CONNECTIONS WITH LONDON GENERAL OMNIBUS CO.'S COUNTRY SERVICES.

The L.U.T. connect at Hounslow with Motor Bus services to Egham and Windsor; at Uxbridge with services to Beaconsfield, West Wycombe and Amersham; at Kingston with services to Weybridge, Woking, Shepperton, Guildford, and Staines. The M.E.T. connect at Edgware with Motor Bus Services to Stanmore, South Harrow, Mill Hill, and Watford; at Barnet with services to Hatfield and St. Albans. The S.M.E.T. connect at Sutton with Motor Bus Services to Walton-on-the-Hill and Lower Kingswood; at Croydon with services to Caterham, Reigate, Epsom, Leatherhead, Esher, Guildford, Sevenoaks, Horsham, Handcross and Uckfield; at Penge with services to Woolwich and Chislehurst.

SMALL DOGS may accompany passengers on the top decks of cars at the discretion of the Conductor, and at owner's risk and responsibility.

SPECIAL CARS may be hired at reasonable rates;

SPECIAL PARTIES. 25% reduction on the ordinary fares is allowed to parties of not less than 15 adults, or 20 children (with attendant adults), the total number of party not to exceed 50 persons. Particulars may be had on application at the Traffic Offices shown below.

LOST PROPERTY. All enquiries for Lost Property found on the Companies' Trams must be made at the Metropolitan Police Lost Property Office, 109, Lambeth Road, S.E.1.

NOTE. Every care is taken in compiling this Guide, but the Companies concerned cannot be held responsible for inaccuracies.

TRAFFIC OFFICES. METROPOLITAN ELECTRIC TRAMWAYS, LTD., Manor House Offices, Finsbury Park, N.4. Tel No.: Tottenham 0077.

THE LONDON UNITED TRAMWAYS, LTD., Manor House Offices, Finsbury Park, N.4. Tel. No.: Tottenham 0077.

THE SOUTH METROPOLITAN ELECTRIC TRAMWAYS AND LIGHTING CO., LTD., Sutton Depot, Westmead Road, Sutton. Telephone No.: Sutton 454.

PASSENGERS ARE REQUESTED TO OBSERVE THE FOLLOWING PRECAUTIONS.

Wait until the Car Stops before boarding or alighting, and when alighting always face the direction in which the car is travelling. Be very careful when Passing Behind the Car—be sure that the road is clear. Do not ride with arms resting on side of top deck—they may be crushed by passing traffic.

55, BROADWAY, WESTMINSTER, S.W.1

Above: The SouthMET timetable for 1928, showing details of the five routes then in operation. *Author's collection*

Below: The SouthMET route map for 1928, which contrasts somewhat with that published in 1906 (see page 37). Sutton, Mitcham and the Crystal Palace were the company's limits; the broken line between West Croydon and Selby Road indicated a route on which through services were operated. *Author's Collection*

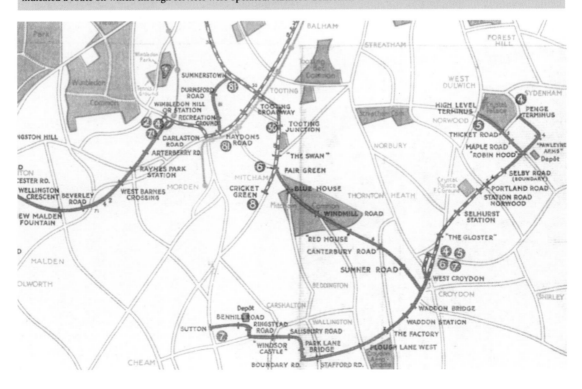

5. 'One of the most important pieces of constructional work in London…'
Conduit construction and completion of the Kingsway Subway

Through the adoption of the conduit system of current collection for its tramways in 1901 the LCC also accepted much more complex engineering than on any other tramway constructed in London. It did not shy away from this and, within a year, was also proposing to use the same system in the first tramway subway to be built in the country.

The LCC's conduit track construction
The complexity of the conduit system masks the fact that there were a number of significant changes made to its construction and installation over the years, as knowledge and experience was gained of its use and operation.

The technology of the conduit system became a topic of much interest, and it was described and discussed at length in journals and texts. The following account is an amalgam of accounts and descriptions of the conduit system, the latest of which was published in 1916:

'The present construction of the centre-slot system on the LCC tramways differs in many details from the original construction installed in 1903. Then the slot rails were fixed to cast iron yokes, to which the track rails were connected by tie-bars. The yokes were spaced 3ft 9in apart and were embedded in concrete, with which the sides of the conduit were also formed. The T conductor rails were carried from insulators, bolted to the flange of each slot rail, the insulators being accessible from the road surface by removable covers.

'The principal features in which the modern construction differs from the original are:

- the use of 'extended' yokes
- the abandonment of removable covers over the insulators
- the use of a slot 1in wide instead of ¾in wide
- the increase in the width of the conduit to 16in

In addition, improvements have been introduced in the construction and drainage of the conduit, and welded joints are now extensively used on the track rails. The yokes are now of two patterns, the 'extended' and the 'short', the former weighing 400lb and the latter 200lb. The extended yokes support the track rails in addition to the slot rails, and are spaced 7ft 6in apart, while the short yokes support the slot rails only, and are placed midway between the extended yokes.

'From a view of the track construction in progress, showing the yokes, rails, and tie-bars … it will be seen that the slot rails, in addition to being tied to the short yokes, are tied to the track rails at each extended yoke,

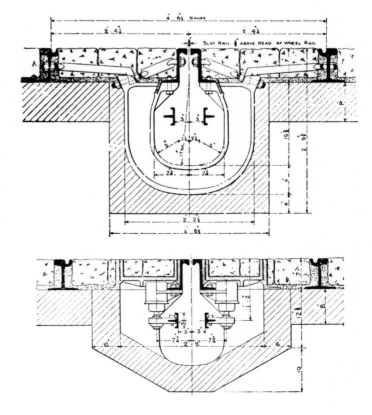

Above right: The LCC's conduit system was based on a regularly spaced series of cast-iron 'yokes' embedded in concrete. Spaced at 3ft 9in intervals, these both formed and maintained the sides of the conduit and, through the use of attached tie-bars, the track gauge. This is a cross-section of the LCC's original form of 'short yoke', used on its first lines in 1903. *Author's collection*

Right: In the LCC's conduit system the current was picked up from a pair of 'T' rails (so called because of their profile), which were carried from insulators bolted to the flange of the rails forming the centre slot between the running rails. This cross-section again shows the LCC's original form of construction for the 'T' rails. *Author's collection*

while the gauge of the track rails is adjusted by taper keys. The joints in the slot rails are arranged at the centre of a yoke, thereby rendering joint plates unnecessary. Where the joints in the track rails are not welded, the ordinary fishplate joint, supplemented by a sole plate consisting of a short length of inverted rail is adopted.

'After the track rails have been lined up and levelled, the yokes are set in 6-to-1 concrete. The centring — by means of which the correct shape is given to the conduit — is next placed in position between the yokes, after which the paving strips (B) and boxes (C), for the insulator pockets, are fixed. The temporary packing blocks under the track rails are then removed and the space up to the flanges of the rails is filled with 6-to-1 concrete.

'The centring was originally constructed of wood, but on straight track a collapsible sheet iron is now used. This is constructed in lengths of 3ft 9in and consists of two sheets, hinged together at the bottom and pressed against the yokes by toggle joints at each end. When the concrete has set, the centring can be made to collapse and can be extracted through openings which have been left for that purpose.

'The paving strips, consisting of lengths of 2¾in x ⅜in wrought iron fitting in grooves in the yokes, are for the purpose of preventing the concrete next to the flange of the slot rail from breaking away. The insulator pockets are placed 15ft apart and the insulators are bolted to the flanges of the slot rails.

'Each insulator pocket is covered by a cast iron plate, which is supported partly on the flange of the slot rail and partly on the concrete and is finally cemented in position. In order to indicate the position of these covers on the road surface, a special square sett or block is placed over each when the paving is laid. With this construction a faulty insulator is accessible only after the paving and the cover plate have been removed. This feature is not considered to be a disadvantage in practice, for, in the first place, the insulators are very reliable and, secondly, the sealing up of the insulator pocket prevents the ingress of mud etc, which was found to occur when the removable boxes were used. In renewing the original track the removable covers are replaced by the modern non-removable covers.

'The conductor rails are of 'T' section, weighing 22lb per yard and consist of high-conductivity steel, having a specific resistance of 4.25 microhms per cubic inch. At each insulator the rail is held in a clip, which is bolted to the insulator pin, the rail being adjusted to the correct position by means of an eccentric washer working in a groove in the clip. Section insulators, consisting of a 2ft gap in the conductor rails, are placed at intervals of half a mile, at which points cables are connected to the feeder pillars and substation. Each end of the conductor rail is flared back 1½in in order to prevent the shoes of the plough from fouling, and at these points each rail is supported by two insulators.

'A plough hatch or box is usually fitted in the slot rails at each section insulator. This consists of two removable plates, each about 3ft long by 4in wide, which when removed leave a fairly large opening over the conduit, through which a plough can be withdrawn.

'In conduit tramways the trackwork at crossovers and junctions is considerably more complicated and costly, since not only must a clear passage be provided under the roadway for the plough, but special points are required for the slot rails as well as for the track rails. The amount of exposed metal at the road surface will be considerable, while the amount below the road will be still greater on account of the extra yokes and gussets required for supporting the extra work.

'The nature of the special work for a double crossing is shown together with that for a crossover assembled on the layout floor at Messrs Hadfields' works.

'The points, crossings, and other parts subjected to wear are constructed of manganese steel. It will be observed that the points in the slot rails are placed after those in the track rails, so that the car will be on the correct road before the plough meets the points.

'The points for the slot rails are of a special design. Each slot point consists of two leaf tongues, which move under protecting covers, the latter being flush with the road surface. The tongues are operated by a lever inserted in the slot at the side of the track. In the straight run-through position one leaf tongue guides the plough past the throat of the point, while in the branch position this tongue moves under its cover plate and the other leaf tongue moves out to guide the plough to the branch track. In order to provide a clear passage for the plough in each direction, it is necessary to insert long breaks — amounting to 12ft or more — in the conductor rails.

'To prevent any accumulation of surface water or mud in the conduit the track rails are drained by drain boxes connected to the conduit through 3in pipes. The conduits are drained into sump pits, spaced at intervals of 120ft along the track with a maximum depth of 7ft 9in. The removal of the mud and the flushing of the pit is performed periodically.'

Completion of the Kingsway Subway

As previously noted, on 12 November 1901 the LCC resolved to seek powers to construct a subway for single-deck tramcars from Theobald's Road, proceeding along the level to Southampton Row where it would descend below street level in a subway and pass along the site of Kingsway — the proposed new street from Southampton Row to the Strand. There the line would turn towards the Embankment, which would be reached near Waterloo Bridge, where the tramway would re-emerge into the open. The subway was completed to Aldwych by June 1904, but the LCC could not obtain the necessary Parliamentary sanction for a compulsory purchase of the land and buildings needed to complete it beyond the

Experience working the conduit system led the LCC to make various changes to its construction, one of the main differences being the development of an 'extended' yoke, shown here. These were twice the weight of the short yokes and used alternately with the latter, at 7ft 6in intervals; they also supported both the running and slot rails. In use these were found to create a much more solid form of track and conduit construction. *Author's collection*

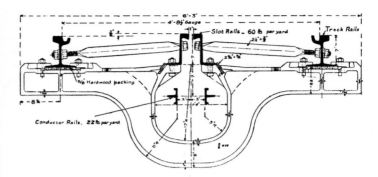

Conduit-track construction in progress, showing the yokes, rails and tie-bars in position. *Author's collection*

After the track rails had been lined up and levelled the yokes were set in 6-to-1 concrete. Here, 'A' is the centring which gave the conduit its correct shape — this was formed from collapsible sheet iron; paving strips 'B' prevent the concrete next to the flange of the slot rails from breaking away, whilst boxes 'C' house insulator pockets — spaced at 15ft intervals — allowing access to faulty insulators by the removal of a special square paving sett which protected a cover plate. *Author's collection*

Strand. As a result the construction was divided into two stages, that between Southampton Row and Aldwych starting first.

Early in 1906 LCC Chief Engineer Maurice Fitzmaurice, who was in overall charge of the project, described some of the difficulties encountered in constructing the first section of the subway: 'The varying levels at which the subway is built show the difference in construction necessary when going along a new street specially constructed, in comparison with crossing existing thoroughfares. It was necessary to dip the rails to a depth of 31ft below the surface of the roadway in Holborn, to avoid existing sewers. At the Strand crossing, the rails have to be kept 34ft below the surface for similar reasons. Under Kingsway no obstructions have to be dealt with, as the sewers, also on both sides, take all gas and water pipes, electric cables, etc. No inconvenience,

however, is caused to the public by dipping under Holborn and the Strand, as the stations are fixed at points where the subway is close to the surface. At both Great Queen Street and the junction of Kingsway and Aldwych, the platform is only 16ft below the street level, so that it is not necessary to provide lifts. … In constructing the subway between Great Queen Street and Southampton Row, very special precautions were taken so as not to damage fine property such as the Holborn Restaurant, and other buildings along the street. … The subway is 20ft wide and 16ft high only so that double-deck cars cannot be run through it.'

The LCC finally obtained the permissions it needed to complete the subway, and to lay down the lines it was to connect to along the Embankment, later in 1906. Work south of the Strand commenced on 11 March 1907. It was divided into three parts:

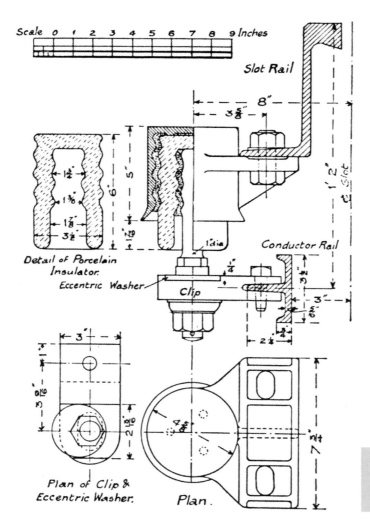

Alteration of Waterloo Bridge abutment to form an entrance to the subway from the Embankment
This consisted of taking down the southern wing of the abutment and constructing a semi-circular arch 22ft 6in wide in place of a smaller stairway arch that existed there. To maintain the architectural features of the abutment the old masonry was taken down carefully, each stone being numbered, and on construction of the new arch this was re-erected. The two west columns and pilaster were moved westward to maintain the spirit of the original design. Afterwards, the only difference between the wing as altered and the abutment's remaining eastern wing was that the arch enclosed between the massive pillars was much larger. The work was designed by the LCC's architect, W. E. Riley FRIBA.

Underpinning of the viaduct supporting Wellington Street
About 360ft of the subway lay under Wellington Street, between Waterloo Bridge and the Strand. The street was built upon a viaduct formed at the same time as Waterloo Bridge,

At each insulator the rail was held in a clip which was bolted to an insulator pin. Use of an eccentric washer allowed the rail to be adjusted to the correct position. *Author's collection*

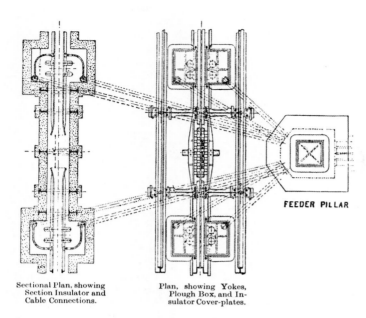

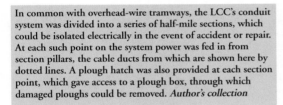

Sectional Plan, showing
Section Insulator and
Cable Connections.

Plan, showing Yokes,
Plough Box, and In-
sulator Cover-plates.

FEEDER PILLAR

Insulator cover plates on the LCC's conduit system. *Author's collection*

In common with overhead-wire tramways, the LCC's conduit system was divided into a series of half-mile sections, which could be isolated electrically in the event of accident or repair. At each such point on the system power was fed in from section pillars, the cable ducts from which are shown here by dotted lines. A plough hatch was also provided at each section point, which gave access to a plough box, through which damaged ploughs could be removed. *Author's collection*

comprised of 16 brick arches on brick piers, the tops of which were, in places, only 4ft below street level. It was not possible to interfere with the surface of Wellington Street, which carried very heavy and continuous traffic. The subway had to penetrate some of these brick piers, so they were examined and found to be springing from timber frames resting on river mud from the old Thames foreshore. Therefore, considerable underpinning was required of these piers before work could commence on the subway, which required cutting openings through them. Then, to spread the load of both the subway and the roadway above as widely as possible, it was decided to form the base of the subway from a raft of concrete, 6ft 6in deep, stiffened with 'I' joist iron beams of 100lb per yard and 24in x 7½in section. Following this stanchions — 17ft 3½in high — were erected on each side of each pier and built up girders were fixed on top of these. Holes were then cut through the piers at the level of the tops of the cross girders — in section 14in by 6½in — and needle joists — in section 8in by 5½in — were put in resting on the cross girders, arranged in pairs and riveted top and bottom. This work was done gradually. Special construction work was also required in the design of the sidewalls. The spaces between adjacent piers at the height of the top of the stanchions were covered in by ceilings; at the Embankment end corrugated toughing being used, elsewhere armoured concrete. The floor of the subway was made concave. For the last 70ft from the Embankment end of the subway cross girders of box form were used, resting on stone blocks let into the brickwork. The tunnel was 16ft wide — the same as the section in Kingsway. Despite all of the difficulties

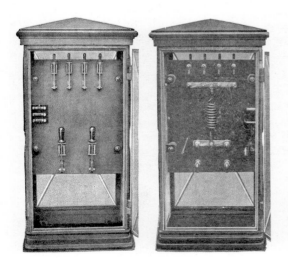

The interior front (left) and back (right) of a typical section pillar. The panel carrying the switches was made of marble or slate. At top are four switches controlling power to the up and down tracks; below are two switches that control the distributors that supply these sections. *Author's collection*

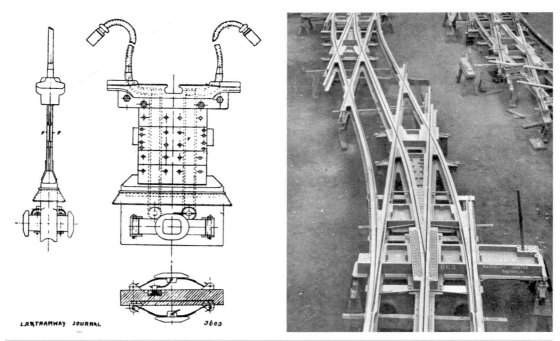

Above left: A standard plough as used on the LCC's conduit system in 1909. Current was collected by cast-iron 'shoes' fastened to a spring by a wedge, as seen in the lower cross-section. The shoes had an average life of around 8,000 miles. Where the plough made contact with the slot rail additional protection was afforded by the use of friction plates, marked 'F' on the top-left section here. These had an average working life of just 3,000 miles. At this time it was estimated that each plough cost £5 7s (£5.35). *Author's collection*

Above right: Special trackwork for a left-hand crossover on the LCC Tramways conduit system, as laid out in the yard of the manufacturer —Hadfields of Sheffield — before delivery. The lighter sections are special manganese steel, which was harder-wearing than ordinary steel. Note the point lever (right) and the provision of plough hatches at both ends of the crossover; these were places where worn or damaged ploughs could easily get stuck! *Author's collection*

Below: More special trackwork at Hadfields — this is a double-track crossing. *Author's collection*

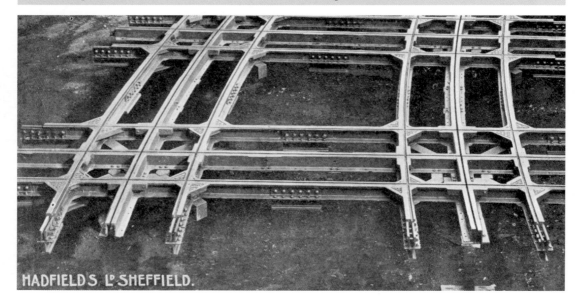

Junction realignment in progress at Gardiner's Corner, Whitechapel, the photograph giving an idea of the complexity of such work on the conduit system. Laid out in the 1870s, the junction brought together the five main thoroughfares of East London — Commercial Road, Leman Street, Aldgate High Street, Commercial Street and Whitechapel High Street. It was named after Gardiner & Co, which firm specialised in military uniforms and children's clothing and whose building, with its distinctive clock tower, dominated the scene. The photograph was taken at 6.43pm on Friday 20 September 1929. *Author's collection*

involved in the work the process of boring for the tunnel did not encounter any problems, notably there being little or no water encountered, which, given the old river mud being worked through, was almost miraculous.

Construction of two tubes under the Strand
Between the northern end of the Wellington Street viaduct and the completed end of the existing subway in Aldwych the new tramlines were carried in tubes similar to those on the tube railways elsewhere in London. To gain access to these tubes at the viaduct end, two circular openings or 'eyes' were formed, each being 17ft in diameter and only 3ft 6in apart. Again, these were constructed without any disturbance to the existing superstructure.

As with the rest of the LCC tramway system the Kingsway Subway used the conduit system of current collection. However, the fact that trams had exclusive use of the subway tunnels and, particularly, that no other

vehicles ran over the paved subway floor, allowed the LCC to adopt a modified and simpler form of conduit construction. The heavy cast iron yokes, described above, were designed to bear the weight of other road traffic, but in the clear absence of this they could be dispensed with. Bulb angle sections, laid in sections, replaced the rigid slot rails, so that the conduit as a whole was much simpler and more accessible for repairs. These bulb angles were laid in 7ft 6in lengths, carried at each end in simple castings bolted to short channel iron cantilevers embedded in the concrete and held down by bolts; their ends being chamfered off to lessen the chance of any fouling by the ploughs as they passed along. The slot was held to gauge by fixed angle bars on either side of the bulb angles, laid in 30ft lengths and jointed by fishplates. Running rails were bolted on to longitudinal timbers of pitch pine, 12in by 6in.

All of the above works were achieved in just 13 months, the entire subway opening on 10 April 1908.

The later history of the Kingsway Subway

LCC Chief Engineer Maurice Fitzmaurice's comment in 1906 that the Kingsway Subway was built to the dimensions it was 'so that double-deck cars cannot be run through it' were perhaps destined to come back to haunt him. By the late 1920s the LCC realised that, to continue to serve its vital role, the subway would have to be enlarged to take double-deck cars. Work to this effect began on 9 September 1929, but it was not necessary to close the subway for the enlargement work until 3 February 1930. This took 11 months, the enlarged subway being formally opened on 14 January 1931.

Scarcely had this work finished before work began to rebuild Waterloo Bridge. The structure was the work of John Rennie and had opened as 'Strand Bridge' in 1817. By the late 1920s it was clear that the bridge had serious structural problems and a decision to replace it was taken in 1935. The bridge was demolished in 1936 and rebuilt over the following years. Giles Gilbert Scott designed its replacement in 1937. It was the last major reinforced concrete bridge built in the UK. The five-span, cantilever bridge had its haunched hollow-box beams faced in Portland stone and, at 1,250ft, became London's longest traffic crossing. Construction coincided with the outbreak of World War 2. Experienced construction workers were moved to the docks so women were brought in to work all along the river, including rebuilding Waterloo Bridge. Despite damage to the bridge from German bombers the predominantly female workforce completed this essential artery in 1942, earning it the affectionate name 'The Ladies' Bridge'.

It was formally opened in 1945. The reconstruction of Waterloo Bridge required the Embankment end of the Kingsway subway to be relocated. This was done in 1937, with the new arrangement coming into use in September that year.

Closure of the Kingsway Subway

The Kingsway subway was closed with the withdrawal of the tram routes using it as Stage 7 of Operation Tramaway on 5 April 1952. The very last trams passed through in the early hours of Sunday 6 July and the occasion was captured on recording tape by the pioneering recordists Jack Law, Geoffrey Ashwell, Victor Jones and John Meredith. Below is a transcript of their recording, which was narrated by John Holmes:

John Holmes: At Aldwych station — one of two in the Subway — it was nearly midnight when one of the last southbound cars passed through …

(Sound of car approaching, passing by and receding into the distance.)

John Holmes: Then, at 12.25am …

The entrance to the Kingsway Subway in Southampton Row at a late stage in its construction but before the service commenced. The hoardings concealed the degree of building work then in progress around the Subway. *Barry Cross collection / Online Transport Archive*

Special all-steel single-deck tramcars were built to work the subway service, there being much concern over the risk of fire in the confined space of the subway's tunnels. This is Type F No 559, one of 16 such cars produced by the United Electric Car Co of Preston. All of the car's cabling was non-flammable and carried in steel casings, and the signal lamps were oil-lit and arranged to illuminate the inside of the cars in the event of a power failure in the subway. *Ian Allan Library*

Type F car No 555 is seen exiting the Kingsway Subway against a backdrop of some of the buildings seen in the previous view. *Barry Cross collection collection / Online Transport Archive*

The first Type F car, No 552, seen in what is probably a posed shot taken at Aldwych station for the opening of the Kingsway Subway in 1906. *Barry Cross collection / Online Transport Archive*

The Kingsway Subway had two passenger entrances, to its stations in Holborn and at Aldwych. The former is seen here with the original style of entrance, in a view taken in 1914. There is remarkably little traffic about and much construction work — the street and subway were contemporaries. *H. O. Dryfern / Author's collection*

The entrance to Aldwych station in 1951, showing the later style. Note that two destinations have been blanked out, following the abandonment of route 31 on 30 September 1950. *Marcus Eavis / Online Transport Archive*

As constructed the southern entrance to the Kingsway Subway was via a portal to one side of the abutment of Waterloo Bridge, tracks joining those on Victoria Embankment in a junction. The details of this are shown here in a diagram published in 1908. *Ian Allan Library*

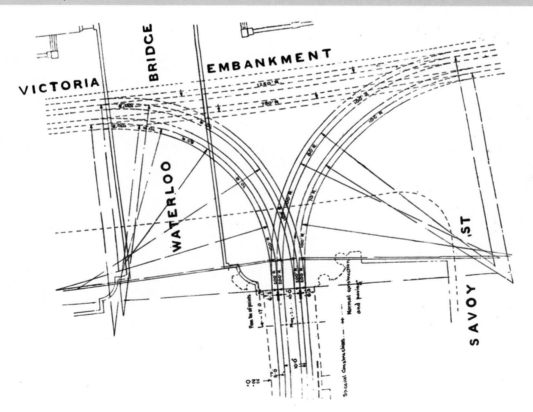

What the original Embankment entrance to the Kingsway Subway looked like. The new stonework is all too evident. Finishing touches are being added to the lamp standards as a Type F car emerges on a trial run through the subway. The trolley plate that these cars carried can be seen on its roof, although none was ever fitted with a trolley pole. *Ian Allan Library*

An animated scene at the same location following the commencement of regular services through the Subway, with a tramway official controlling traffic as a car emerges onto the Embankment. Note the presence of at least three 'BEWARE CARS CROSSING' notices. *Barry Cross collection / Online Transport Archive*

g Subway, Thames Embankment, London.

Jack Law: Here comes the last northbound 35 car through the Subway arriving at Aldwych station. Car No 185. Packed to capacity and quite a large crowd on the platform — seeing it off …

(Sound of car approaching, and cheers from the crowd)
John Holmes: As on previous occasions, London Transport officials were joined by local civic dignitaries. And, shortly before the last tram was driven through, the Mayor of Holborn, Councillor Ling Cooper, had this to say …

Cllr Ling Cooper: It's been a very great privilege to drive the last tram through the Kingsway Subway. I remember well the first one that went through about 45 years ago, and I feel that this marks another phase in the traffic problems of London. The trams have served a very useful purpose, but of course they come to the stage of obsolescence like we all do — and we can only hope that the new means of transport provided in place will be of adequate service to the public, as in the past …

John Holmes: Ever faithful, a sizeable group of Londoners waited patiently at the northern end where the track rose to street level by way of a 1-in-10 gradient. And, at a quarter to two …

Jack Law: And here comes 185 …

(Sound of car descending gradient, with wheel-flats chugging on the rails)

Jack Law: … the two white lights at the top are now horizontal, telling a tram now standing at the top that he cannot yet enter the Subway. And now they've changed to diagonal which means that the 185 is now in Holborn station — and the track is now clear for the last car …"

(An unidentified 'E/3' car descends the approach ramp in Southampton Row, entering the Kingsway Subway.)

John Holmes: And a few minutes later …

Jack Law: And here comes the last car. The blind window frame hanging down. No 184 …

(Sound of car braking and drawing to a halt.)

London Transport Inspector: That's it boys — that's it …

Voice in distance: Clear the gates … Come on … Further down … Further down …

(Sound of car braking.)

Jack Law: He's stopped a little way down the Subway whilst photographs are taken. The Inspector is closing the gates for the last time …

John Holmes: But in fact the gates were reopened to admit a London Transport official motor car to follow the last tram.

Afterlife
In 1953 London Transport used the Kingsway Subway to store 120 withdrawn buses and coaches in case they were needed for the Coronation and in 1955 it was used to represent a railway tunnel in the film *Bhowani Junction*. A film company then offered to take over the whole subway as a studio, but this was rejected on account of the fire risk. Repeated questions in Parliament kept the issue alive, but in 1955 London Transport invited applications to use the tunnel as a store for non-inflammable goods and finally leased it in October 1957 to S. G. Young & Co of Blackfriars for use as a machine-parts store. In June 1958 the LCC wanted to take over the subway and create an underpass for light traffic beneath the Strand and Aldwych in an attempt to deal with traffic jams which often extend right across Waterloo Bridge. John Mowlem & Co was awarded the contract for the conversion in July 1962, and work started on the 15-month contract. This was completed on schedule, and the new Strand underpass opened on 21 January 1964.

A cross-section showing the arrangement of tracks in double tunnels, which summarises many of the constructional points made. *Ian Allan Library*

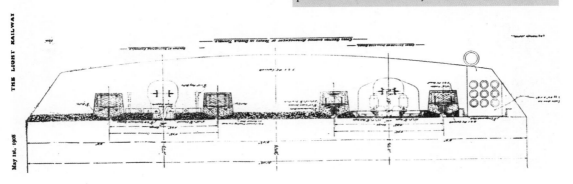

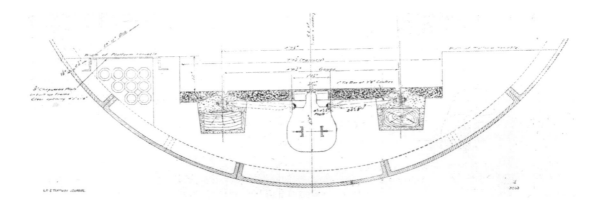

Above: A cross-section showing track construction in the single tunnels in the vicinity of Aldwych. *Ian Allan Library*

Below left: 'Thirty-ones' abounded at the reopening of the Kingsway Subway following its reconstruction for operation by double-deck cars. On 14 January 1931 specially painted 'E/3' car No 1931, showing route 31, was the official first tram through the Subway, being seen here *en route* to the opening ceremony. *Barry Cross collection / Online Transport Archive*

Below right: 'E/3' No 1931 prepares to enter the Subway from the Embankment during the reopening ceremony on 14 January 1931. Footage of the occasion, described later, shows the car entering with both trolley booms forward. *Barry Cross collection / Online Transport Archive*

More excited crowds in the newly enlarged Kingsway Subway on 14 January 1931, with official first car No 1931 seen at right. *Barry Cross collection / Online Transport Archive*

Another photograph taken on 14 January 1931, showing cars in normal service. The lamps are very stylish. Note the camera bag beneath the notice board (bottom left). *Barry Cross collection / Online Transport Archive*

Above left: The reconstructed Aldwych station in 1931, which was described as being 'bright with colour and light'. *Ian Allan Library*

Above right: Holborn station was similarly appointed to Aldwych, as apparent from this photograph taken around the time of the Subway's reopening. *Barry Cross collection / Online Transport Archive*

Below: An unidentified 'E/3' car leaves the southern portal of the Kingsway Subway beneath the reconstructed Waterloo Bridge to gain the tracks along the Embankment. *Marcus Eavis / Online Transport Archive*

Class E/3 car No 1948 emerges from the Kingsway Subway in Southampton Row. *Marcus Eavis / Online Transport Archive*

An unidentified 'E/3' car descends the approach ramp in Southampton Row, entering the Kingsway Subway, as No 184 would have done on the very last run. *Marcus Eavis / Online Transport Archive*

Holborn station more than 50 years after the last tram used the Kingsway Subway. Most of the infrastructure remains intact, the tracks are even *in situ* beneath the shallow material covering them and can be seen here in relief. *Nick Catford*

Looking down the Kingsway Subway south of Holborn station. A crossover in the track is still visible. In the gloom at the end is the beginning of the construction of the Strand Underpass. *Nick Catford*

6. '... a scheme for dealing expeditiously with the cars ...'

The LCC Tramways' Central Repair Works

The LCC's Central Repair Works owed its existence largely to the Tramways' Chief Officer, Aubrey Llewellyn Coventry Fell. He was born in Llangollen in 1869, 'Coventry' being his mother's maiden name. Trained as an electrical engineer, he succeeded Alfred Baker as General Manager, after the former was lured away to run the tramways in Birmingham, on 20 October 1903. In addition to his LCC position, Fell was also President of the Municipal Tramways Association. He was awarded the CBE in 1920 in the Civilian War Honours, which recognised the part played by civilians during the Great War, and retired in 1924, being succeeded by Joshua Bruce. Aubrey Fell died on 4 October 1948, aged 79.

Aubrey Llewellyn Coventry Fell (1869-1948) was Chief Officer of the LCC Tramways and President of the Municipal Tramways Association. Coventry was his mother's maiden name, and its inclusion made his already impressive roster of names all the grander. *Ian Allan Library*

An idea of Fell's role in bringing about the building and development of the works is conveyed by an account published in September 1909: 'Mr Fell perseveringly kept the matter before the Highways Committee until authority was given to proceed with the requisite building and equipment.' This was between 1904 and 1906. The LCC's original intention had been to repair and renovate its fleet in small shops attached to each depot. After deciding to build a central works, a part of New Cross depot was converted into a temporary repair works, the all-too-evident inadequacy of the size of this serving to underscore Aubrey Fell's insistence upon a central facility.

New Cross sufficed until a suitable site could be found for the repair works. This had to be centrally situated, from a tramway viewpoint, and inexpensive, many being rejected 'owing chiefly to their high intrinsic value'.

Combining the account referred to above with another detailing the works, published one month later, provides a glimpse of its progress to that date.

The Central Repair Works was needed to deal with the large amount of work, which resulted from the operation of more than 1,000 cars. Its 6.9-acre site was at Charlton, just off the Greenwich Lower Road, conveniently accessed from the north side of the Thames via the Blackwall Tunnel and adjoining the Angerstein Wharf of the South Eastern & Chatham Railway, from which it was proposed to construct a siding.

By 1909 only 3.5 acres of the site was in use. One reason for this — and possibly also why it had a low 'intrinsic value' — was that the soil was found to be 'of a somewhat unsuitable character.' Trial borings had revealed that it was 'largely composed above the level of what was evidently a part of the old river bed at a depth of from 12 to 15ft below the ground level of made ground'; therefore 'it was thought advisable to carry down concrete piers to the ballast bed to support the steel stanchions'.

The general layout of the works was shown in a ground plan, reproduced here. The workers entered through a series of double turnstiles, which registered both the number who went in and the number who went out. A standard-gauge railway ran around the site and in the yard, along which cars were hauled by a small steam locomotive supplied by Andrew Barclay & Co. Great store was placed upon the fact that this locomotive was the only steam-powered device on the site; everything else was electrically driven by current drawn from the tramways' Greenwich power station.

W. E. Riley, the LCC's superintending architect, designed the buildings. They rested upon concrete rafts, about 1ft 6in thick, and were of steel with plain brick outer walls. The south facing slopes of the roof were covered in Bangor Countess slates whilst the north facing slopes were glazed with roughcast wired glass. At mezzanine level above the truck and machine shops were galleries containing smaller machinery; these had pitch pine floors.

By the autumn of 1909 the works had a capacity to deal with the overhaul of 600 cars per annum, but an extension to give greater capacity was already in hand. Apart from routine maintenance, a major driver for the works were the Metropolitan Police regulations, which required the bodywork and painting of each car to be thoroughly renovated once in every 12 months. The LCC took advantage of this requirement, opting also systematically to overhaul and put into first-class condition all the mechanical and electrical equipment of the cars. The works was arranged to allow and ensure the regular and synchronous progression of the cars through the various shops, over a period of two weeks.

A map of the LCC Tramways as at 1 August 1909, showing the lines built, authorised and those still-horse operated. *Ian Allan Library*

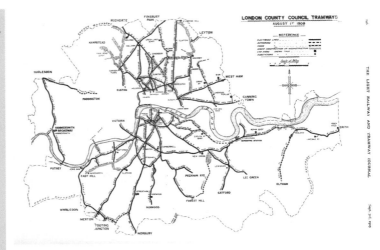

A ground plan of the Central Repair 'Depot' — as it was known — showing its proximity to the South Eastern & Chatham Railway and the main divisions within the buildings occupying the 6.9-acre site. *Ian Allan Library*

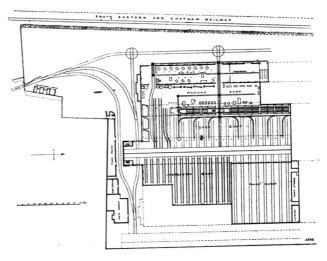

A plan showing the galleries at the Central Repair Works, which mostly accommodated smaller machinery. *Ian Allan Library*

A sample of the exemplary system of paperwork that accompanied the passage of cars through the Central Repair Works to ensure that there were no difficulties or delays in processing the work. This sheet relates to Class D car No 323. *Ian Allan Library*

Tramcars were processed through the Central Repair Works according to the following routine. The works superintendent issued a form requesting the cars due for renovation each week to be transferred from their running depot to the repair works on a Sunday night. As the cars entered the gateway they shed their ploughs at a special run-out and were then coupled to the works' Barclay locomotive which drew them to the western end of the site and onto a traverser. From here they were moved to an available road in the Inspection Shop. The following morning the cars were inspected and a detailed list was compiled of the works required on each. While a car was still in the Inspection Shop the brake rigging, trucks and associated equipment, including the bottom halves of the gear cases, were disconnected; it would then be drawn back onto the traverser, and the body lifted clear of the trucks by two pairs of pneumatic jacks. The traverser next moved the detached trucks to a point immediately under one of the lighting wells provided in the floor of the gallery above. Here the motors were lifted by a travelling crane and taken to the Motor Overhauling Shop (housed in one of the galleries), the trucks going to the Truck Shop on the western side of the traverser pit. Mounted on a temporary truck, the bodies were taken to the Body Shop. Work on the trucks and motors generally took four days and set the timetable for the work on the bodies. At the end of this period the cars were reassembled prior to going into the Paint Shop. This was cleared of its finished cars every Sunday, and the overhauled and reassembled cars were placed in readiness for the painters to start work on the following morning; their work, plus that of the varnishers, took a week. If all went to plan, each week's output of renovated cars was ready for inspection by noon on the second Saturday following the day upon which they were received at the works.

Class E1 car No 1120, 'the latest type of LCC car' at the time that the Central Repair Works was described in September 1909. One of a batch of cars numbered 1052-1226, it was built by Hurst Nelson. *Ian Allan Library*

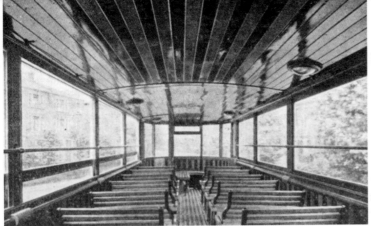

The individual shops and areas of the Central Repair Works at this date were as follows:

Smith's Shop — 130ft by 34ft, fitted with 13 hearths and equipment including two 5cwt pneumatic power hammers, one double-head grinder, a 10cwt drop-hammer and an annealing furnace. Special attention was paid to the extraction of fumes and smoke by employing stoneware ducts connected to the draft pipe of the hearths. The shop began working in June 1908 but when visited in September 1909 was virtually dirt-free.

Machine Shop — 143ft by 43ft, fitted with eight lathes, a power press, one plain milling machine, a high-speed four-spindle drill, seven other drills and slotting and screw-slotting machines, the centre of the shop being occupied by fitters' benches.

Wheel Shop — 65ft by 117ft, fitted with three high-speed tyre-boring mills, three high-speed tyre-turning lathes, a 150-ton wheel press, pneumatic lifting hoists, etc. It was estimated that steel tyres lasted 50,000 miles on driving wheels and 56,000 miles on pony wheels.

Truck Shop — 195ft by 46ft, with 14 working tracks and a capacity for 28 pairs of trucks, fitted with two 5-ton overhead cranes. The plant includes equipment for recovering oil from the cotton waste used in the shops. In a year it processed 20,000lb of material and reclaimed 12,000 gallons of oil.

Traverser — 293ft by 43ft, equipped with a traverser by Applebys Ltd, operated by Westinghouse motors and equipped with four 10½in pneumatic car-lifting jacks. The track gauge was 13ft 6in, and the traverser drew power via a standard car plough.

Inspection Shop — 156ft long, 52ft of which was 37ftwide and the remainder 75ft wide, with inspection pits under each road, including 15 tracks with pits.

Paint Shop — 104ft by 112ft, ventilated and warmed, provided with adjustable platforms and having a paint-mixing and grinding shop, eight tracks (each capable of accommodating three cars) and powered roller shutters that could separate this shop from the traverser pit.

Tool Room — 46ft by 15ft; tools were served out over a counter and signed for by each workman.

Tool Stores — 39ft by 16ft, equipped with 1,270 bins and a drawing rack.

An end view of LCC 'E/1' car No 1120, showing how smartly turned-out these cars were by the Central Repair Works. The destination blind shows 'NAG'S HEAD'. *Ian Allan Library*

A general view, southwards, inside the Smith's Shop at the Central Repair Works. Note the internal narrow-gauge rails to ease the movement of parts around the shop. *Ian Allan Library*

The western wall of the Machine Shop at the Central Repair Works. The narrow-gauge lines are again visible. All of the machines were belt-driven off a main-line shaft mounted high on the wall. *Ian Allan Library*

The northeast corner of the Machine Shop at the Central Repair Works. Here the line shafting and belting is more evident. The main machine to view has a bevelled drive, the three diameters of pulley wheel enabling the speed the machine worked at to be varied. On the line shafting above, each drive had two wheels. One was an idler wheel, on but not attached to the shaft. Moving the belt on to this wheel effectively turned the machine off. *Ian Allan Library*

Finished Part Stores — 39ft by 16ft, with 1,750 bins.

General Stores — equipped with 6,720 bins for parts obtained from outside manufacturers, and a 20-ton weighbridge.

Galleries — (Small) 197ft by 20ft, equipped with small lathes, drills and tools, plus a pattern store; (Large) 275ft by 48ft, including a Testing Room, Plough Shop, Motor Shop, Controller Shop and armature- and coil-winding machines.

Offices — housing a general clerical office, timekeeper's office and a Superintendent's Office.

Mess & Cloak Rooms — a two-storey building with a kitchen on the ground floor, with seating for 284, and 560 metal lockers.

Yard — including areas for storing coal, coke and iron and various offices for the gatekeeper and the Pay Office. Here arrangements were in place for paying 600 workers in five minutes!

The depot was electrically lit throughout, inside and out, using 60 Sunrae flame-arc lamps, and all departments and offices were linked by an internal telephone system.

Works systems
To accompany these arrangements, systems were also devised to monitor Works' labour costs and give a clear indication of the status and cost of a job at any time during the progress of the work through the shops. It was based on a series of forms:

Above: The Truck Shop at the Central Repair Works was equipped with these machines for recovering oil from the cotton waste used in the shops. In a year it processed 20,000lb of material and reclaimed 12,000 gal of oil. *Ian Allan Library*

Below: The Inspection Shop at the Central Repair Works was equipped with 15 pits. This diagram shows an inspection pit in cross-section. *Ian Allan Library*

Below right: A view inside the Paint Shop at the Central Repair Works showing the painters' adjustable scaffold. The only car identifiable is Class D No 387 of 1904. *Ian Allan Library*

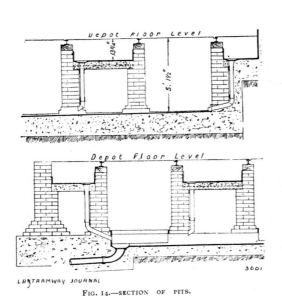

FIG. 14.—SECTION OF PITS.

Form No 1 — the initial issue from the Rolling Stock Superintendent's Office authorising and instructing the Works to proceed. This bore a job number in its top right-hand corner that was used on each form to be used subsequently with the job.

Form No 2 — the Works' Superintendent's instructions to the foremen, instructing each to do their part of the work.

Form No 3 — the workmen's daily time sheet, on which the time spent on each job was recorded.

Form No 4 — the requisition for the necessary material from the Stores.

Form No 5 — the credit ticket for the finished articles received at the Stores.

Form No 6 — a folder card in which all of the above forms, except No 3, were held, together with any other written material necessary in connection with the job. The outside pages were for entering costs and quantities.

In this way the whole history of the job was recorded on the folder card. Every Monday a further form — No 7 — was sent to the Rolling Stock Superintendent, detailing the previous week's output and costs.

Right: The body of No 402, the first of the LCC's 'E'-class cars, undergoing extensive work in the Central Repair Works. *Barry Cross collection / Online Transport Archive*

Below: The Truck Shop at the Central Repair Works in 1922. Three car bodies are in view, along with various trucks and the Small Gallery (left) and Large Gallery (right). *Barry Cross collection / Online Transport Archive*

Above left: 'E/1' car No 1773 of 1922 being lifted off its trucks at the start of a routine maintenance through the Central Repair Works. *Barry Cross collection / Online Transport Archive*

Above right: Another 'E/1', No 1584 of 1912, has been raised clear of its bogies, which are being wheeled out to go to the Truck Shop, in February 1932. *Barry Cross collection / Online Transport Archive*

Below: Also in February 1932 a pair of 'E/1s', Nos 1800 and 1805 of 1922, are under lamps in the Paint Shop at the Central Repair Works whilst the lacquer on their paintwork dries. *Barry Cross collection / Online Transport Archive*

7. 'Undercover All The Way'
Tramway publicity

Publicity was key to all of London's tramway operators and, in addition to the usual timetables and system maps, which all such undertakings produced, they also promoted their services and service innovations through often striking artwork displayed on posters and leaflets. Despite this being 'disposable' and very ephemeral material, both the LCC Tramways and the Underground Group employed artists of considerable ability, some of whom were just at the start of what turned out to be very illustrious careers.

The LCC Tramways was at the forefront of this and, being part of a much larger authority, was able to draw upon the talent within the LCC Central School of Arts and Crafts. The building, now the Central St Martin's College of Art & Design, stands on the corner of Theobalds Road and Kingsway. It was built between 1905 and 1908 to a design by LCC architect A. H. Verstage, but this was influenced by the School's founder William Richard Lethaby (1857-1931). Lethaby was an architect and architectural historian whose ideas were highly influential on the late Arts & Crafts and early Modern movements in architecture, and in the fields of conservation and art education. He was appointed Art Inspector to the Technical Education Board of the newly formed London County Council in 1894 and, largely due to his influence, became the founder of the Central School of Arts and Crafts in 1896. The Central School of Arts and Crafts was one of the first buildings to be erected along the newly forming Kingsway, beneath which ran the Kingsway Subway.

During the 1920s the LCC Tramways also employed the services of the Ralph & Brown Studios and the talents of its founding partners: Rickman Ralph and Pieter Irwin Brown. The latter was born in Rotterdam in 1903 and travelled widely in Europe and Africa before moving to London, where he worked for the Leigh Breton Studio before setting up a design business in partnership with Rickman Ralph. Brown worked extensively for the LCC Tramways and also for the Underground Group and later for the London, Midland & Scottish Railway and Great Western Railway. In the 1930s he travelled to Indonesia, Japan and China, where he produced Japanese-style woodblock prints. He moved to the USA in 1940 and worked under the name Pieter van Oort, settling in New York in 1946.

Notable artists who produced publicity material for the LCC Tramways included:

- Freda Beard (*fl*1920-1940) — portrait painter and commercial artist. Her work appeared on a variety of poster designs, including commissions for the British Empire Exhibition of 1924 and for the Royal Mail Line shipping company. She also designed posters for the Underground Group between 1921 and 1926 and twice exhibited at the Royal Academy.

- J. L. Carstairs ((*fl*1900-1940) — also produced posters for railway companies, notably the London & North Eastern Railway, and went on later to design book dust wrappers and cover art for magazines such as the *Radio Times*.

- Tony Castle (1891-1971) — designed posters for the LCC Tramways and worked extensively for London Zoo, producing a series of striking posters during the 1930s.

- Lance Cattermole (1898-1992) — also designed railway posters and carriage prints and continued to do so in the era of British Railways.

- Muriel Jackson (1901-1978) — portrait painter and wood engraver.

- Frank Marsden Lea (1900-1967) — prolific poster artist.

Other artists who worked on publicity material for the LCC Tramways were Leslie S. Abbott, Rene Blair, F. W. Farleigh and Leslie R. Porter.

Much of the artwork produced by the above artists and others to promote London's tramways has transcended the fleeting moment they were created for to become highly collectable. Their posters are reproduced and originals are listed regularly in the catalogues of fine art houses. Examples of their work appear on the following pages.

Above : A full-page LCC Tramways advertisement promoting 'A Mile of Sightseeing for 1d'. *Author's collection*

Below : '2d All the Way' — the front of a flyer introducing the LCC's off-peak low fare in 1921. The fare was available on all weekday cars timed to arrive in Central London between 10.30am and 4.30pm or departing from there between 10am and 4pm. The facility was extended to Sundays from the summer of 1929. *Author's collection*

Above: London trams in an advertisement. In May 1912 the British Thomson-Houston Co Ltd promoted its tramcar meters by declaring that they were 'Supplied to the London County Council Tramways'. The car shown is a stylised 'E/1'. *Ian Allan Library*

Below left: '1/- All Day' — an eye-catching graphic to promote the LCC Trams all-day ticket, introduced in 1925 as a Sunday and Bank Holiday special but quickly extended to become an everyday facility. *Author's collection*

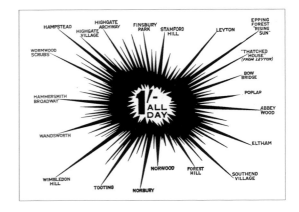

Top left: It wasn't just the LCC that produced promotional material. This is the cover from a *Tramway Trips & Rambles* guide, part of the 'Walker Miles' series produced by the MET and LUT tramways. A man assists his female companion over a stile as a tram waits in the background. *Author's collection*

Top right: 'Southwark Bridge — The New Tramway Connection with the City'. The cover of a small flyer, with an illustration by Oliver Burridge dated 1925.

Below: 'Cheap Fares for the Million by L. C. C. Trams' — a block advertisement, dated January 1926, summarising all the LCC's cheap-fares initiatives. *Author's collection*

OUT and HOME	MIDDLE HOURS	ALL DAY	CHILDREN UNDER 14
5ᵈ 6ᵈ 8ᵈ RETURN (WITH TRANSFERS) FOR SINGLE JOURNEYS OF **3ᵈ 4ᵈ 5ᵈ** RESPECTIVELY By the regular use of Return Tickets a tramway passenger saves from 26s. to 52s. a year. By availing himself of Transfer facilities he saves time as well. EVERY DAY	**2ᵈ** ANY DISTANCE ON ANY ONE CAR LONGER 1d STAGES On cars *Leaving* the Central London Termini between 10.0 a.m. and 4.0 p.m. . . *Arriving at* Central London Termini between 10.30 a.m. and 4.30 p.m. Longest distance for 2d. Victoria Embankment—Abbey Wood 13½ miles. Average distance for 1d. 2 miles. MONDAY TO FRIDAY EXCEPTING PUBLIC HOLIDAYS	**1/-** RIDE AT WILL BOARD ANY CAR CHANGE ANYWHERE There are 164 miles of tramway in the 1/- area, within which the passenger may, on the day of issue, Board any car; Change at any point; and make as many journeys as desired with only one ticket. The passenger travels at will, saving himself energy and keeping expense to a minimum. EVERY DAY	**2ᵈ** ANY DISTANCE (WITH TRANSFER FACILITIES) 1d. FOR ADULT'S 2d. FARE DURING MIDDLE HOURS OF THE DAY MONDAY to FRIDAY (Excepting on Public Holidays) The fare for a Child under 14 is **1ᵈ** ANY DISTANCE ON ANY ONE CAR

Cheap Fares for the Million by L.C.C. Trams

January, 1926

FOR CHEAP FARES AREA—P.T.O.

Board the First Car

Saving of passengers' time is the aim of the board-the-first-car plan, which now applies to midday fares of **2d ALL THE WAY** to and from Central London

The facility practically eliminates waiting for cars.

On most routes there is always a car within sight.

In many cases money as well as time is saved.

L.C.C. TRAMS

Left: "Board the First Car'. On 11 April 1927 the LCC Tramways introduced a transfer-ticket system in conjunction with the '2d All the Way' tickets to encourage people to get on the first available tram and change to the route they wanted at specific transfer points. These were all listed on the tickets, which were up to nine inches long as a result! These three ladies seem to have got the hang of it. *Author's collection*

Right: 'London's Tramways to the West End' — the lure of London's West End nightlife promoted by a nifty bit of artwork produced by the Ralph & Brown Studios in October 1928. *Author's collection*

Below left: Under Cover All the Way' — a stylised depiction of LCC trams on the Embankment in a linocut by artist F. W. Farleigh, who has used the medium's stark contrasts to maximum effect. *Author's collection*

Below right: 'Travel Quickly — Read in Comfort'. Front and back of an LCC leaflet emphasising the 24-hour service provided and showing the time bands during which its various fares were available. This was the work of the Ralph & Brown Studios in 1927. *Author's collection*

LONDON'S TRAMWAYS TO THE WEST END

Frequent Services of well-lighted Cars

Reading and Smoking in Comfort

Travel under Cover all the Way

L.C.C. Tramways,
Victoria Embankment, W.C. 2

J. K. BRUCE,
General Manager.

UNDER COVER ALL THE WAY

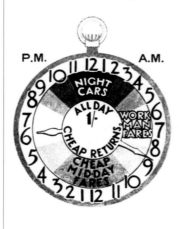

Service unceasing is rendered by L.C.C. Tramways, which work for **24 Hours per Day** and provide the widest facilities

TRAVEL QUICKLY READ IN COMFORT

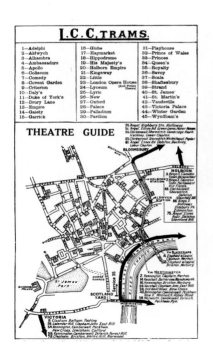

Above left and left: 'The Comfortable Way in All Weathers'. Front and back of an LCC Tramways flyer promoting trams as a means of visiting the theatre. The pencil sketch shows a long queue waiting patiently in the rain for a car to pull up. *Author's collection*

Above : A colourful perspective painting of Kingsway to promote the 'Direct Services of Pullman Trams between North and South London via Kingsway'. The car emerging bottom right is 'E/3' No 1931. *Author's collection*

A 1/- All-Day Ticket
on London's Tramways
is available for
unlimited journeys
on 200 miles of route
on the day of issue

FIXTURES FOR LONDON

FOOTBALL

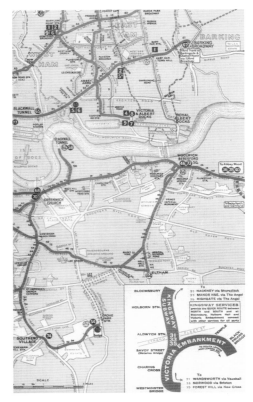

Above left: 'Fixtures for London — Football' — another simple but effective graphic from the Ralph & Brown Studios, in September 1931. Our goalie has saved the 1/- All Day! *Author's collection*

Above right: A bold and striking panel from the inside of the map, promoting the Kingsway Subway services. *Author's collection*

Right: LCC Tramways map and timetable. The LCC produced one of these per month, each with a different design of artwork on the cover. This one, from May 1933, features York Water Gate at Charing Cross — 'Now separated from the Thames by the Victoria Embankment & public gardens'. *London's Transport Museum*

8. '… a complete revolution in the appearance of London's tramcars'
LCC 'E/3' and 'HR/2' tramcars and LCC experimental car No 1

Beginning in 1922, Christopher Spencer, Tramways Manager of the London & Suburban Traction Co Ltd, began experiments to improve the speed and comfort of the tramcars in the London United, Metropolitan Electric and SouthMET fleets. The eventual outcome of this work would be the 100 'Feltham' cars introduced in public service from 5 January 1931. At the LCC Tramways a mass modernisation programme — termed 'Pullmanisation' — was also carried out on all but 200 cars in the fleet, these being of older designs deemed unsuitable for the process, which mainly involved upholstered seats and brighter interiors; this was carried out between June 1926 and March 1930.

Unable to refurbish its older designs of car, the LCC Tramways decided to replace them. At its meeting on 28 July 1928, the LCC Highways Committee received a report in connection with the question of substituting new tramcars for 292 cars of the older Classes A and D bogie types that were not deemed suitable for Pullmanisation. This was independent of the same committee's deliberations upon 50 special new cars contemplated for services on hilly routes. Overall, it was agreed that 237 additional new cars would be required. Eight months later, at its meeting on 26 March 1929, the Highways Committee approved in principle the purchase of 300 new cars and proposed as a first step the immediate purchase of 150, including the 50 of special type for hilly routes. On 23 July, the LCC approved a capital estimate of £453,000 in respect of the 150 cars referred to and by March 1931, 136 of them were

already in service. At the same time it was noted that 115 of the older Class A and D cars were still licensed for service but that these were 'in such a condition that it is not practicable to maintain them, even for such purposes as they are now made to serve, for more than a few months. The cost of necessary running repairs thereto is increasing, and they are not capable of earning the same revenue as is obtained with the cars of the newer types.'

An estimate of car requirements was also presented, calculated as at 31 March 1931:

Maximum number of cars required for service (including spares)	1,707
Number of modern type cars which will then be available in the Council's fleet	1,602
New cars provided by Leyton Corporation (but not available by 31 March 1931	50
Ultimate inclusive total of modernised fleet as authorised to date	1,652
Deficiency of cars against requirements	55

The impending completion of the authorised tramways from Grove Park to Eltham (opened in two stages on 1 October 1931 and 30 June 1932) placed a further requirement for 13 additional cars, thereby increasing the overall car deficiency to 68. Against this, the Highways Committee considered using Class HR/2 cars,

Side elevation of the 'E/3' tramcar as published on 18 July 1930. *Ian Allan Library*

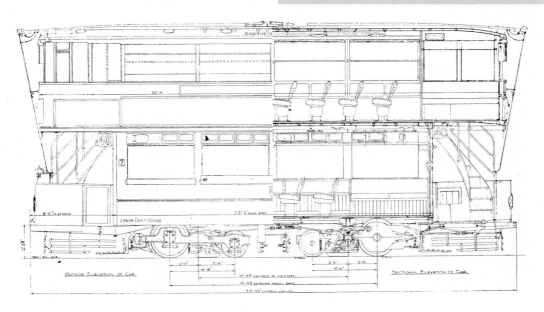

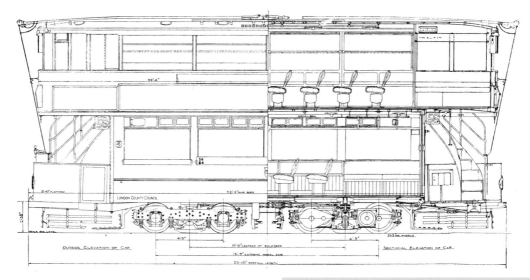

Side elevation of the 'HR/2' 'hill-climbing' tramcar.
The bodywork for these and the 'E/3' cars was practically
identical. *Ian Allan Library*

introduced on the Dog Kennel Hill routes, to work the
Highgate Hill service. To this end, the Chief Inspecting
Officer of the Ministry of Transport had been consulted
on the matter and had been in agreement, subject to
points of detail concerning the braking on the cars.
Thus, by withdrawing the remaining Class M four-wheel
cars from these two hilly routes and replacing them with
Class HR/2 cars would, through their combined
advantages of higher speed and greater seating capacity,
reduce the overall need for cars by eight and the overall
net deficiency thereby to 60. Changes in working
practices at the Central Repair Works at Charlton had
also substantially reduced the time cars spent in there
from the original two weeks, and therefore increased the
number of days in each year during which a car was
available for service. As a result of these deliberations,
the Highways Committee decided that the supply of 60

additional new cars of the HR/2 class would be sufficient
to modernise the fleet and to meet all demands currently
foreseen. To achieve this they recommended extending
the Council's existing contract for 150 new cars and that
the cost of these was not to exceed £174,000. An
additional £7,200 was to be provided to meet the

The first public view of an LCC Tramways 'HR/2' car, 'One
of the Eight-wheeled Cars which are replacing the single-truck
vehicles on London's hilly routes'. The car bears the Council's
coat of arms and is showing route 56 (Peckham Rye–Victoria
Embankment), which ran along Dog Kennel Hill, Dulwich.
Ian Allan Library

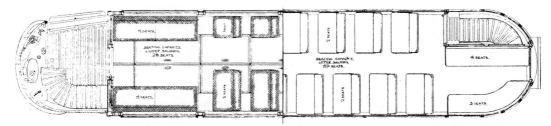

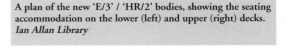

A plan of the new 'E/3' / 'HR/2' bodies, showing the seating accommodation on the lower (left) and upper (right) decks. *Ian Allan Library*

possible cost of supplementary brakes which the Ministry of Transport might recommend for the Highgate Hill cars, and a further £1,300 to meet incidental costs for engineering, inspection and testing, making an estimated total cost of £182,500.

The first of the new Class E/3 general use 'Pullman' cars entered service during the first week of June 1930 — just in time for the Whitsun holiday traffic and press and public reaction was unanimous: '... the bodies are of a standard design, and are even more attractive than the 1,450 Pullman tramcars already operated by the LCC. Metal has been largely used in the construction, while special super-size structural plywood has been used for the main roofs. The interior of the upper saloon is five inches wider, which gives more "elbow room" to passengers, and permits of a wider gangway between the seats. Ventilation has been improved in both saloons, and the windows in the upper saloon can be opened and closed at will by passengers. Linoleum has been used for flooring.'

As the finishing touches were being made to the cars at the Central Repair Works at Charlton the trade press were given an opportunity to inspect the new vehicles: 'The bodies of the two types of cars are practically identical and have been constructed to seat comfortably 74 passengers, 28 being accommodated in the lower

saloon and 46 on the upper deck. One extra seat has been gained in the lower saloon, partly as a result of it having been necessary, in order to secure additional space for supplementary safety devices, to increase the length of the four corner longitudinal seats to accommodate four persons each instead of three, which has necessitated the doing away with of one row of transverse seats.

'A very great improvement has been effected in the ventilation of the lower saloon. In addition to four "Ashanco" ventilators — one at each corner — the rear units in either direction being "intake" and the front ones being "exhaust", the ventilators above the windows are of a novel pattern. These ... are known as the "all one way" type and are controlled by a hand lever placed at the centre of the saloon on either side. Each ventilator is vertically hinged at the centre and when the control lever is placed in the direction of travel one half of each vent opens to face the direction of travel. At the turning point of the journey the conductor moves the control levers in the opposite position and the half vents, which have been open, now close and the other halves open facing the reverse direction. When the lever is placed in a central position both halves of each ventilator are closed. By this method it is impossible for the fresh air which enters at the front ventilators to pass out again through any rear vent at the side of the car, so that all used air is drawn through the rear saloon doorway. During inclement weather when these main ventilators are closed the air can be changed without draught every two minutes through the "Ashanco" arrangement described above.

A view of the lower saloon of 'E/3' car No 1912 showing a new design of ventilators over the main windows. *Ian Allan Library*

'The ventilation in the upper saloon is primarily effected by the "Windsor" half-drop side windows which can be operated at will by passengers. Additional ventilation is assured by means of "Venturi" air-extracting units and the ventilating scheme embodied in the roof lamp fittings, whereby the heat from each lamp is utilized to assist the air extraction.'

As noted above, the upper decks were five inches wider than other cars', this being 'due to the fact that a very special design of structural framework has been embodied and produced as a series of interchangeable castings in "Alpax" metal. This type of framework is now being made the standard for upper-deck construction, and identical top covers will be fitted to the older cars when substantial repairs or reconstruction is necessary. The flooring has been improved by the provision of non-slip "battleship" linoleum … [which] substantially facilitates cleaning of the vehicles, particularly in bad weather. The roofs of both upper and lower saloons have been constructed with SCT structural plywood, each in one piece only, and finished normally 3/8in thick. … it is only recently that such boards of a suitable size have been procurable. The firm responsible for the manufacture of this material is the Tucker Armoured Plywood Co Ltd, Crayford, Kent.

'The ceilings of both saloons have been finished in white enamel and handrails have been provided; … [on] the upper deck [these] extend on either side and for the full length of the gangway from end to end, while the similar rails fitted in each corner of the lower saloons are provided with neat leather handholds. … Such pillars and rails as are employed for the subsidiary framing to carry the main saloon windows, sliding door, etc., are of selected Moulmein teak. The exteriors of the main saloon bodies at each end are panelled in Honduras mahogany, the sides being steel plate. The external panels of the upper deck consist of sheets of 22SWG-thick high-tensile aluminium alloy fitted each in one complete width.

'The underframes and side structures of the bodies are constructed from rolled and pressed mild steel sections, electric welding having been generally employed to secure the units comprising each structure, whilst at certain points where exceptional local loads have to be met supplementary bolts or rivets have been used. The panelling of the lower saloon is structurally component with the side framing of the car and consists of specially selected rolled mild steel plates having a tensile strength of 28 to 32 tons per square inch. Non-splinterable safety glass has been used for certain windows and panels in such parts of the car as are most liable to damage.'

Hurst Nelson & Co Ltd of Motherwell built the 100 'E/3' bodies, those for the 50 'HR/2' cars being built by the English Electric Co Ltd at Preston. The trucks for the 'E/3' cars were Class AA double-bogie sets of the plain-bushed centre-bearing swing-bolster type with cast steel side frames and were generally in accordance with the existing standard trucks for the LCC's Class E and E/1 cars. Their axleboxes — and those of the Class 6 trucks supplied for the 'HR/2' cars — were equipped with roller bearings. Written in the contract with their manufacturer — the Electro-Mechanical Brake Co Ltd of West Bromwich — was a stipulation that the bearings 'were to be made by firms who have secured a sound reputation for such products operated satisfactorily over extended periods of use, under conditions of intensive service … equivalent to those maintained during the last five years within a radius of 25 miles from the traffic centres of London, Manchester and Birmingham.' The bearings were required to be capable of giving a service life of at least 500,000 miles, during which they should not require lubricating more frequently than once in every 20,000 miles. SKF bearings, manufactured by the Skefko Ball Bearing Co Ltd, of Luton, were used. With the Class 6 trucks used on the Class HR/2 cars, the equal-size wheels, of 2ft 2½in diameter, ensured 100% traction efficiency. Their wheelbase was 4ft 9 in and the approximate distance between their pivotal centres was 11ft. The combined effect of the four traction motors was to be capable of accelerating a tram loaded to not less than 20 tons at not less than 3ft per second up to 12mph, a speed which could be maintained on a gradient of up to 1 in 11.

A view of the upper saloon of No 1912, showing the new type of windows installed. *Ian Allan Library*

Left: A front three-quarter view of No 1912, showing its crisp clean lines. The car was photographed at the Central Repair Works in Charlton. *Ian Allan Library*

Below: A Class AA truck for the 'E/3' cars, which had SKF roller-bearings in its axleboxes. *Ian Allan Library*

Above right: A Class 6 truck for an 'HR/2' car. The effect of the four traction motors was to accelerate a tram loaded to not less than 20 tons at not less than 3ft per second to a speed of 12mph, which could be maintained on a gradient as steep as 1 in 11. *Ian Allan Library*

Below: LCC Tramways 'E/3' car No 2002 working route 54 when newly into service. *Barry Cross collection / Online Transport Archive*

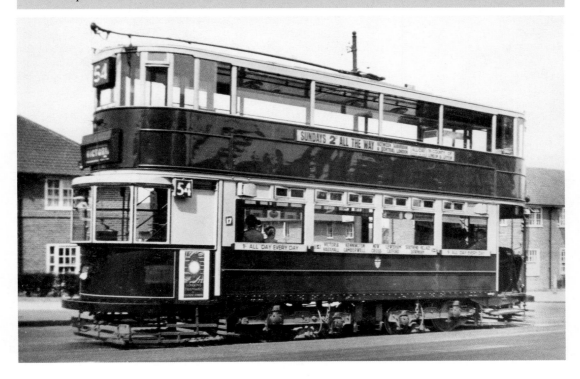

Above left: 'HR/2' cars Nos 101-59 were not fitted with trolley booms as they were not intended to work off the conduit system. No 139 is seen here working route 11 (Highgate Village–Moorgate) in Pemberton Gardens, Holloway. *Barry Cross collection / Online Transport Archive*

Above right: Reflecting its steep gradient, Dog Kennel Hill, Dulwich, was laid with four tracks — two in each direction. In this early-1950s view 'HR/2' No 1877 is seen working route 60 as a sister car passes by on route 58. *Barry Cross collection / Online Transport Archive*

Below: This view of an 'HR/2' working route 58 up Dog Kennel Hill, Dulwich, ably demonstrates the steepness of the gradient. *Barry Cross collection / Online Transport Archive*

LCC Experimental tramcar No 1

Just before Christmas 1929 the LCC Highways Committee announced that it had authorised expenditure of up to £5,000 in the 1930/1 financial year for the construction of an experimental tramcar embodying enclosed vestibule ends designed as an integral part of the structure, comfortable seating, adequate lighting, ventilation, etc. The committee also expressed a view that 'It is desirable that the construction of the vehicle generally shall be carried out by the direct employment of labour in the tramways department.' This last statement is probably an acknowledgement of the pressure Government was applying to large employers, such as the LCC, to create employment.

In early January 1930 the press was agog with further details of what was billed as the 'New Super Tram for LCC System'. However, it seemed that '… ideas of the rolling stock staff have not yet been advanced beyond the drawing stage, but they are sufficiently definite to show that the new super-car will differ very materially from the cars of today'. Integral vestibules, reported above, remained in favour and, '… provided police sanction can be obtained, will enable some twenty more standing passengers to be carried during rush hours than is possible now'.

Other design ideas that ultimately got no further were also hinted at, such as that '… of a central entrance, with doors to close automatically, from which a central stairway would lead to the top deck. An alternative plan also under consideration is that of a stairway from the extreme rear of the car. An argument in favour of this proposal is that passengers entering from the rear and not from the side would be afforded protection from passing traffic. … The Tramways Department are endeavouring to solve two problems by giving the utmost comfort to passengers, and by moving the rush-hour traffic in the most speedy way possible.'

The new super tram was given pride of place in the LCC fleet by being numbered 1, formerly allocated to the first in the Council's original fleet of 100 Class A cars which opened its electric traction service in 1903. These had all been withdrawn by 1931. The new No 1 was ready by May 1932 and was inspected at Charlton by members of the LCC's Highways Committee in the first week of that month. It may have been seen on test beyond Charlton, but its first definite 'public' appearance was on Thursday 19 May 1932, when it was used to convey some of the delegates to the Tramways, Light Railways & Transport Association's 22nd Annual Conference, which was held in London from 18 to 20 May, from the Embankment to the Central Repair Works at Charlton.

A press preview had also been held at Charlton the previous week, and the praise lavished upon the new car was effusive. As one journalist put it, 'In recent months we have described and illustrated several new experimental tramcars which have been built by British municipalities, and in each case we have been tempted to apply to them that greatly misused phrase "the last word". But just as each of these cars had apparently exhausted the ingenuity and skill of its designers, as surely did the next descriptive article reveal new ideas and angles of approach in design. In last month's issue [February 1932] we described and illustrated the new experimental car, which the Edinburgh Corporation had put into service, and that car did indeed seem to be the last word in design and equipment. Below we describe a new tramcar, which has been built by the LCC Tramways Department, and which incorporates many novel features which are due in great part to the fertile mind of Mr T. E. Thomas, the General Manager. Under the leadership of Mr G. F. Sinclair, the new Rolling Stock Engineer, coupled with the

The original caption to this photograph of LCC No 1 reads: 'Front view of the new LCC tramcar. Note the excellent effect of the stream lining'. *Ian Allan Library*

enthusiastic coordination of other members of the engineering staff, the new car … embodies many modifications of existing practice and in our opinion attains a very high level of artistic excellence.'

No 1 was built throughout at the Central Repair Works in Charlton. The improvements it embodied were based upon the experience gained from the 'HR/2' equal-wheel bogie cars, of which 112 had been built since the type first entered service in April 1929. The new car had been built longer and wider than the 'HR/2s', its working design having been planned to take advantage of all the permissible clearance allowed between vehicles of the same type passing on adjacent curves, as sanctioned by the latest memorandum from the Ministry of Transport covering operation within the Metropolitan Police area. The new car's principal working dimensions were:

Overall length	36ft 0in
Length of body, including cabs, at floor level	34ft 9in
Width outside (lower saloon)	7ft 3in
Width outside (at cantrail of upper saloon)	6ft 11in
Height from rail to top of lower saloon floor	2ft 5in
Height from rail to top of roof at centre	15ft 3in
Height from rail to top of trolley base cover plate	15ft 11in

Net seating capacity was for 66 passengers — 28 in the lower saloon and 38 in the upper.

Structurally, the new tramcar consisted of a rectangular steel box, of which the sides formed deep self-contained truss girders and comprised the equivalent of all normal side panelling, complete with the sole bars. This steel structure continued above the level of the lower saloon roof to the height of the bottom rails, which supported the upper-deck window frames, at which point the main all steel structure ended. The whole 'steel box' was welded together, except in a few places where parts or panels needed to be removed regularly or in an emergency.

To save weight the window frames in the upper portion of the car were formed from Alpax aluminium castings, based upon the experience gained in using this material in the new 'E/3' and 'HR/2' cars and in experiments with car vestibules. The roof was formed from a single sheet of structural plywood, shaped by streaming under hydraulic pressure; the extreme ends were more Alpax castings. Similarly, the upper-deck floor was also formed from a single sheet of structural plywood, ⅜in thick.

On the lower deck the floor was at a uniform level throughout, including the vestibules and drivers' cabs; it was covered with 'battleship' linoleum. The lower saloon had four large windows, the two end ones capable of being dropped for extra ventilation. The upper saloon was fully glazed 'so that passengers have full opportunity to witness passing items of interest *en route*'.

As the upper saloon was intended primarily for smoking passengers four 'Colt' ventilators with adjustable outlets had been fitted to the centre upper ceiling panel. Both saloons were lit artificially with units comprising a reflector and decorative glass panel cover.

An immediately noticeable difference between the experimental car and its predecessors was the seating. This was all padded and upholstered in moquette with edges of hide or grained rexine, with the exception of 'bench' seating above the main entrances, but these did have seat backs, which, in practice, gave 'the comfort of an individual'.

Access to the upper saloon was by means of an easy staircase of ample width, the two bottom treads of which were placed parallel to and immediately opposite the main car entrance, so that 'incoming passengers will easily and automatically divide into separate streams for the main and upper saloons'.

Much of the striking modern design of LCC No 1 was owed to the availability of new materials, notably a modified aluminium/silicon alloy called 'Alpax', which was made by Lightalloys Ltd of Willesden Junction. This advertisement accompanied an article featuring No 1, published in the *Electric Railway, Bus & Tram Journal* dated 13 May 1932. *Ian Allan Library*

Passengers could communicate with the driver and conductor by any one of an ample number of electric bell pushes located in convenient positions on the ceilings, in the stairwells and doorways. Separately, the driver and conductor could communicate by means of atmospheric air bells with signalling points to and from each cab and at each entrance.

The experimental car also had a number of safety features, including a headlight capable of being focussed for use as a fog lamp, an 'overtaking traffic' warning-lamp signal fitted on the nearside and connected to the brakes, an air-controlled double screen wiper and air-operated sanding apparatus.

Attention had also been paid to passenger flow. The entrance doors, combined with safety lifting steps and side lifeguards, were all air-operated and under the driver's control. In normal operation the car would work with the rear doors open and step down whilst those at the leading end would be closed, allowing the vestibule space to accommodate standee passengers comfortably. The doors were in pairs, divided in the centre.

The exterior of the car was painted Royal blue, with ivory-white streamlining designed to accentuate the lines of the bodywork. At certain points gold lining enriched the white paintwork. Protective parts liable to traffic damage were finished in black, making them less obvious than on other cars. Window rails, handles and auxiliary fittings were in polished stainless or chromium-plated steel.

On the interior, the lower saloon had a proportion of its woodwork left in its natural grain. The seating moquette had an antique blue foundation, relieved by occasional overlays of salmon pink between two shades of fawn, the hide used on the fronts and edges of the seat covers being a deeper shade of blue. The 'battleship' linoleum on the floor was of a deep rich shade chosen to throw into higher relief the colours embodied in the seat coverings and general finish. Heating grilles were bronze, whilst the rest of the fittings in the saloon and staircase were polished stainless or chromium-plated steel. The ceiling was finished in a dead matt white stippled enamel relieved by stainless steel mouldings. All remaining lower saloon woodwork was painted an attractive shade of lustrous Chinese blue.

Space in the staircases accommodated plate glass panels to display Council posters. Decoration in the upper saloon was simplified by the large amount of glass the design afforded. The ceiling was the same as in the lower saloon, and the sides below the windows were covered with a stout type of non-scratchable rexine cloth in a shade approximating to that of the lower saloon. The moquette used on the seating was similar but not identical to that in the lower saloon, and the floor was again covered in 'battleship' linoleum.

Above left: The interior of the lower saloon of LCC No 1 was described as 'beautiful'. A combination of moquette and rexine was used for the seats. Note also the concealed lighting. *Ian Allan Library*

Left: The interior of the upper saloon of LCC No 1. The absence of roof supports allowed an unobstructed view from front to rear. *Ian Allan Library*

Above: A view of the conductor's platform of LCC No 1, showing the air-operated doors fully open and the retractable step. *Ian Allan Library*

Right: The staircase entering the upper deck of LCC No 1 near the 'B' end — note the individual backs to the curved bench seats at the end of the car. *Ian Allan Library*

The car's main equipment was as follows:

Brakes — wheel (air- or hand-operated) and track (air- or magnetically operated)

Trolley booms — two, to avoid the need for a boom to be swung in traffic

Motors — 4 x 30/35hp mounted one to each axle, permanently coupled in series on each truck

Drive — single helical gear

Trucks — 4ft 9in wheelbase

All of this combined to produce a car that could accelerate, from rest, at 3ft 6in per second up to 35mph, or up to 15mph up a gradient of 1 in 11.

Delegates to the Tramways, Light Railways & Transport Association Conference, held in London from 18 to 20 May 1932, inspected the new car when they visited Charlton Works on 19 May. The editor of the *Electric Railway, Bus & Tram Journal* believed that after their inspection the delegates would agree '… that tramways, far from being obsolescent as was suggested in the Final Report of the Royal Commission on Transport, are inherently capable of providing for their patrons greater travelling comfort and a larger measure of safety than any other form of street vehicle'.

By this time the travelling public had also had a chance to experience the new car as it entered public service on the Kingsway Subway routes 31, 33 and 35 in the week commencing 9 May 1932.

LCC No 1 was intended to be the forerunner of a series of similar cars, probably incorporating slight modifications based upon experience gained through its operation — but this was never to be. Only 14 months after its introduction the LCC Tramways passed to the LPTB, which was more in favour of trolleybuses.

LCC No 1 in service on route 22 at Manor House in 1932. These days it is quite astonishing that on the side should be painted 'Tramcars provide Comfort for Reading and Smoking'! *Ian Allan Library*

9. '... replacement by buses will not improve the transport situation ...'
The campaign to save London's trams

Although ultimately powerless to prevent the abandonment of tramway operation in London, some were not prepared to see them go without at least putting up a fight. A lot of the opposition came from the Light Railway Transport League (LRTL) and was expressed through the pages of its journal *The Modern Tramway*, plus those of various local newspapers which covered South London, notably the *Kentish Independent* and the *Kentish Mercury*. One of the most vociferous of the campaigners at this time was Alan J. Watkins (1926-93). Ten years after he died his widow, Ann, pulled together his tramway papers from that time to produce '*The Campaign to Save the London Trams 1946-1952*', from which the following is taken.

Despite the best efforts of the LCC Tramways, the Underground Group and the London Borough tramway operators, trams were more or less doomed from the formation of the London Passenger Transport Board (LPTB). Section 23 of the London Passenger Transport Act 1933, which established the LPTB and vested in it the assets of London's tramway operators, stated:

'Subject to the provisions of this section the Board may abandon either in whole or in part any tramway forming part of their undertaking. At least three months before the date on which any such abandonment is to take effect the Board shall give notice of the proposed abandonment and the date upon which that abandonment is to take effect to the highway authority responsible for the road on or above which the tramway is laid or erected.

'Upon any such abandonment the Board may, and if so required by the responsible highway authority, shall, within a period not exceeding three months from the date upon which the abandonment takes effect or such longer period as the highway authority may allow, take up, remove and dispose of the rails, conduits, paving setts, posts, poles, wires and other works used or provided for the purpose of the tramway so abandoned (in this section collectively referred to as "tramway equipment").

'Subject to the provisions of this section, the Board in any such case shall forthwith fill in and make good the surface of the road to the reasonable satisfaction of the highway authority to as good a condition as that in which it was before the tramway equipment was laid or erected.

Once the tramway has been abandoned, the Board ceases to be charged for any expenses incurred: and for the repairing of the roads.'

A 'Feltham' car working route 8 moves away from Victoria terminus. This was the only tram terminus situated in the main entertainment and shopping part of Central London. As can be seen, the road here is wide, and two islands were provided for boarding the trams, the crossover allowing trams to reverse into the more southerly of these. Route 8 would be withdrawn on 6 January 1951. *Marcus Eavis / Online Transport Archive*

'Feltham' No 2140, working route 16 to Croydon and Purley, makess its way through Elephant & Castle. This was one of the longest routes in London, the journey taking around 75 minutes; it would be withdrawn on 7 April 1951. The splendid Burton's building (left) and the *South London Press* building (behind the tram) would be swept away when the area was redeveloped in the 1960s. A planned redevelopment in the 2010s has been put on hold. *Marcus Eavis / Online Transport Archive*

In a speech entitled 'Moving the Londoner', delivered in May 1949, LPTB Chairman Lord Latham said that 'The urgent problem for the future is the replacement of the tram in South London. Trams are to be substituted by another form of transport, namely buses. Buses will provide a service to the public, which, in the altered circumstances of today, will be no more costly than the trolleybus. The bus, not being attached to fixed wires, is completely mobile. A fixed form of transport will be unsuited to the changing plans and highway structure of London.'

At the same time Sir Cyril Hurcomb, Chairman of the British Transport Commission (BTC), expressed his thoughts on the abandonment of trams in South London, stating that he decision for the replacement of the South London trams by buses had been taken after prolonged consideration of the alternatives:

- Buses would give greater co-ordination with existing bus routes

- Extension of the routes will better serve traffic objectives

Sir Cyril stated that the problems of tram retention were as follows:

- The electricity-distribution system would have to be expanded

- The cable system would have to be expanded

- Electrical equipment and cables were in short supply, and delivery dates a long way ahead

- The erection of trolley poles and overhead wires would have to include Westminster Bridge and the Embankment, which were both close to the Houses of Parliament; this would result in a loss of civic amenity in the heart of the capital

The principle arguments for the abolition of trams were:

- London Transport did not like them

- Buses were cheaper to run and were more flexible

- Trams were regulated, but buses were not

- 21-year tram leases were about to expire

- Vehicles and track were in need of renewal and repair

Writing in the Journal of the Institute of Transport for November 1953, Charles F. Klapper reported: 'After the formation of the LPTB in 1933 it was decided to extend the trolleybus route to the rest of the South London system to Bexley, Erith and Dartford, where the track and cars were worn out. When the South London scheme came up for review in 1945 after the Second World War, the motor bus was favoured instead of the trolleybus. At that time (before taxation changes) diesel fuel cost less than traction current. In 1946 a bus scheme for London was prepared. In the last stage, 114 buses replaced 162 trams. [In all,] 737 trams were taken out of service and were replaced by 768 buses.'

It was against this background that some sought to reverse an irreversible situation. The 'Tramway

On a very wet day another 'Feltham', No 2128, is seen on route 18 in North End, Croydon, passing Whitgift Hospital (right) and about to pass the large range of Allders department store, founded in 1862. Route 18 would be withdrawn on 7 April 1951. *Marcus Eavis / Online Transport Archive*

On another rainy day ex-Croydon Corporation car No 384 waits at Thornton Heath terminus in Whitehorse Road. Severed tracks, which formerly extended the route back to the centre of Croydon, can be seen to the right of the tram. Route 42 was another destined to be withdrawn on 7 April 1951. *Marcus Eavis / Online Transport Archive*

On 8 July 1951 ex-LCC No 591, one of the first series of 'E/1' cars, negotiated new trackwork on a temporary bridge at Deptford Creek. These tracks came into use on 30 July 1949 and would be abandoned upon the withdrawal of route 70 on 10 July 1951. *Marcus Eavis / Online Transport Archive*

Non-trolley 'HR/2' No 146 caught working route 56 in September 1951 at Peckham Rye, this being the view southeast from Nunhead Lane. The route would be withdrawn on 6 October 1951. *Marcus Eavis / Online Transport Archive*

Another non-trolley 'HR/2', No 120, in Lordship Lane, Dulwich, working route 58, which came in for much criticism in the pages of the *Kentish Mercury* in 1951. *Marcus Eavis / Online Transport Archive*

Development Council', with headquarters at Peckham, was formed in 1949 to try to save London's trams. It staged a leaflet campaign that advocated modern single-deck trams able to carry about 80 passengers. There was also a South East London Action Group, in which the late Alan Watkins was involved, which held regular meetings at the Progress Hall in Eltham. The following is a typical salvo from one of the campaigners — a letter from Alan F. Deverell published in the *Kentish Mercury* for 19 May 1950 entitled 'Buses for Trams — A Question of Capacity':

'Sir —
   I do not know whether the public of South London have considered the difference in the number of passengers which will result from the conversion of trams to buses, but the outlook is rather gloomy. In a recent "Mercury" article it was stated that 800 trams are to be replaced by nearly 1200 buses. The great majority of trams are 74-seaters, with a total carrying capacity of 59,200, but the new buses only carry 56, which means the total capacity of 1,000 buses will be 56,000. Assuming all vehicles are on the road at the same time, 3,200 passengers will be left behind. Add to this the fact that the buses almost certainly will not cover exactly the present tram routes but will no doubt extend beyond, it is easy to see now that more buses will be needed to provide the same service. What are these other 3,200 would be passengers going to do to get to work? Go by Underground? Impossible, there is not an adequate system in any part of South London; there is, of course, the Southern Electric, but these trains are grossly overcrowded as it is. To provide a complete and

satisfactory service, I think at least 1,200 buses will be needed to replace the trams. We in South London, especially the South East, must see to it that we are not left behind, as so often has happened in the past.'

In addition to opposing the withdrawal of the existing tramways the Tramway Development Council proposed new lines with new vehicles. It announced one such scheme in 1950 — a radical plan for a rapid-transit tramway running both at surface level and below ground along a corridor from Purley and Croydon to a major new transport interchange at Kennington Oval. Here the 'rail coaches' would connect with Northern Line tube trains to the City and West End and also with a future extension of the rapid transit line to Victoria, Marble Arch and Paddington.
   The line would use reserved tracks for street running, with tunnels and flyovers to avoid traffic pinch points. Stopping places would be spaced further apart than with other modes of street transport, provided with small platforms and shelters for use in adverse weather. More elaborate stations would be provided at rail-interchange points, including a substantial underground tram station in central Brixton where Acre Lane and Coldharbour Lane cross Brixton Road and Brixton Hill. An interchange station in a cutting below street level was to give interchange at Oval tube station.
   Twin-coach trains would be made up of long single-deck carriages (rail coaches) with a high power-to-weight ratio and rapid acceleration. Plenty of space would be provided for standing passengers, whilst resilient rubber wheels would reduce noise. Grass and flower borders would help make the reserved track sections more attractive and neat fencing

would ensure pedestrians did not stray into the path of
high-speed trams. A more elaborate development of this
scheme covering more of south London appeared in
The Modern Tramway for July 1950.

Regrettably none of thme to pass. The scheme also
suffered from two handicaps: in a period of austerity
there was no money for major new capital investment
and it did not emanate from within London Transport.
Nonetheless its technical conception was first class.

The *Kentish Mercury* proved a good forum for the
debate, and letters appeared regularly into 1951.
The examples quoted below illustrate the need for
good public transport in London:

'Sir —

When the LPTB took over the running of buses and
trams after smashing all private enterprise, they gave us a
slogan: "Cheapness and Efficiency". Those in Lewisham
who have memories now emit a hollow groan every time
they recall — as they must do — the very many efficient
services we used to have under private competition.
There are no prizes for the answer, but can anyone tell
me if there is any worse service anywhere in the world
than a 58-service tram. Perhaps the LTE would like to
explain to the hundreds of people who wait anything
from 15 to 25 minutes at King William's Walk,
Greenwich, in all weathers after working all day,
their idea of "Cheapness and Efficiency". When the LCC

ran the cars along that route we had two services
(Nos 58 and 62) and a rush-hour service (No 50).
We have repeatedly been told that the LTE are taking the
trams off the roads and substituting three buses for every
two trams, but I invite the people to consider carefully
what will happen when they do. During December we
had a fair example of different classes of weather and
what happened? Buses were practically at a standstill in
fog and frost. The people who on one night waited over
half an hour for a bus opposite the Town Hall, Catford,
could give an answer to that. The trams were still moving
occasionally, although perhaps not in the direction that
everyone wanted. The South East of London is being very
badly served and everyone could demand that we should
have the services we are entitled to, and if the LTE cannot
supply them, someone else should be allowed to. A tube
should at once be considered and started. This would serve
a dual purpose of providing an atom bomb shelter and a
passenger transport service in any weather.

A. B. Stewart'

In reply to A. B. Stewart's letter, published on 16 February 1951, George Dodson-Wells, Chief Public Relations Officer for the LTE, wrote:

'Sir —

I would assure you that we are doing all we can to give travellers in this part of London the best possible facilities. As regards tram route 58, to which your readers particularly refer, a service of 15 trams an hour is scheduled to operate on this route during the peak periods, with six extra trams to Catford, at the busiest times, in the evening. When fully operated, this service is ample for the requirements of the traffic. The trouble to which Mr Stewart refers, which is greatly regretted, has occurred because the route has been affected by acute staff and rolling stock difficulties, which depleted services on a number of occasions. Supervision is given by an official to the queues at King William Walk, Greenwich, on all possible occasions to ensure that the services are operated to the best advantage. A separate queue for route 58 faces the queue for routes 36, 38, and 40 to make conditions as easy as possible, and, when the situation permits, trams are turned back towards Catford and Forest Hill. Perhaps I may add that the trams on route 58 are to be replaced by buses in October this year and that all the trams in South-East London will be replaced by the end of 1952. We trust, despite your correspondent's fears, that this will contribute a noticeable improvement to transport facilities in that area.'

One terminus of route 58 was the entrance to the Blackwall Tunnel in Tunnel Avenue. Here non-trolley 'HR/2' No 118 waits to return to Victoria. Route 58 would be withdrawn on 6 October 1951. *Marcus Eavis / Online Transport Archive*

Kingsway Subway

As the inevitability of tramway abandonment in London became apparent, some sought to retain what they regarded as the best features of the system, particularly the Kingsway Subway. The following extract is taken from an article in the *Kentish Independent* for 12 August 1949 entitled 'They want Trams under the Streets':

'The members of the Tramway Development Council, anxious to stop London from discarding its tram system, visualize modern subway tram systems bigger and better than the Kingsway Subway, capable of carrying thousands of passengers in silent comfortable high-speed trams. These could speed safely through the tunnels at 25-second intervals. Subway tramways are cheaper to build than tube railways. It says that its system could be installed for an average cost of £200,000 a mile, and no costly signalling equipment would be required. A tube line costs more than £1,500,000 a mile.

'Although the proposed scheme would mean that subways would have to be built under the streets in congested districts, the trams would come to the surface where there is sufficient room, and run on

lines fenced off from the adjacent roads. In this way, it is claimed, the trams would offer no obstruction to other traffic.'

In response, the leader of Woolwich Borough Council said: 'As I don't think the proposal would be acceptable to the LTE, I have not given it any further consideration.'

In a letter to *The Star* for 18 October 1949 entitled 'Tramway Subways' S. P. Harris wrote: 'One of the most useful and efficient methods of underground travel — the Kingsway tram subway from Bloomsbury to the Embankment — may be abandoned when South London's trams are replaced by buses. The principle of tramway subways is one that has not been exploited sufficiently in London.'

Routes 33 and 35, the latter using the Kingsway Subway, were withdrawn on 5 April 1952. The impending abandonment of the subway became the focus of much criticism in the letter pages of local newspapers in the years leading up to the inevitable. Here 'E/3' No 182 is seen working route 33 at the Angel, Islington. *Barry Cross collection / Online Transport Archive*

The Kingsway Subway's last winter as 'E/3' car No 1999 works up the ramp in Southampton Row through the snow. Amongst the comments made ahead of its closure was: 'Abandonment of the Kingsway tram subway means three surface bus routes, which may disorganise traffic in this area'. *Marcus Eavis / Online Transport Archive*

Alan Watkins was also strongly in favour of retaining the Kingsway Subway. Writing in the *Evening News* for 27 June 1950, he said: 'In suggesting that London trams should be replaced by some form of railway, reader A. P. Tatt, writing in *The Evening News* on 26 June 1950, apparently realises that replacement by buses will not improve the transport situation but will worsen street congestion and slow down services. Abandonment of the Kingsway tram subway means three surface bus routes, which may disorganise traffic in this area. Retention of the subway and development of a system of reserved-track tramways and subways would, therefore, be beneficial.'

Abandonment

In 1952, at the time of the abandonment of the trams, the edition of *The Economist* bearing the ominous date of 5 July included an article entitled 'A street car named defunct', in which were listed the reasons for the final tramway abandonment that day:

- Trams were not allowed to run in the West End

- There was a general prejudice against trams

- Access of trams into the City was limited

- With its narrow streets, London was not like Continental cities

- The Tramways Act 1870 stipulated that the road between the rails and pavement 18in either side had to be maintained by the operating powers

- Housing developments which were away from tram routes made tramway extension expensive

- Continental cities did not have the same amount of urban sprawl, hence tramways were economically viable

The following table was then included to show that the cost of a bus seat was equal to half the cost of a tram seat:

Receipts for trams	Excess running costs	Vehicle costs		
		Trams	*Buses*	*Trolleybuses*
£2,360,000	£1,250,000	£8,000-£11,000	£3,500-£5,000	£6,000

Effects of abandonment

Not long after the final trams ran in July 1952, Alan Watkins wrote the following account of the repercussions of their abandonment:

Recently London Transport has stated that the abandonment of tramways has resulted in a big improvement in traffic conditions. This has not been the experience of several independent observers (except in the lane of New Cross Gate), and it is suggested that, where there has been some slight improvement (as at Kennington), the same could have been achieved by road and track improvements which, in most cases, have been long delayed. The following examples are selected:

1. New Cross Gate

Considerable delays have always been experienced owing to the trams' running in and out of the depot, and the changing of crews which was often carried out with anything but smartness. This point is unsatisfactory for a depot, but the following improvements could have been made:

- A double triangular junction into the depot, eliminating the necessity for reversing cars running in

- Quicker crew changes

Even so, little improvement could have been effected by the use of buses had not many of the replacing buses been operated from Rye Lane garage, Peckham. This has

quite naturally led to coincidental improvement at New Cross Gate, but much of the trouble has been transferred to the narrowest part of Peckham High Street, almost on top of the busy Rye Lane junction.

2. Elephant & Castle

Improvement here can be attributed to the new traffic arrangements, whereby road traffic is now controlled by the general flow of the trams.

3. Brixton

The position here is steadily worsening as the trams are removed. Large traffic blocks are prevalent, and conditions are so bad that the buses are forced to load and unload in the middle of the road. This represents deterioration as tramway passengers could use a loading island. Some years ago, an independent body proposed a tramway subway under Brixton. Had this scheme been followed, considerable improvement would have been effected, as the following services could have been removed from the street (based on existing routes):

Tram	Now Bus
8-20	57
22-24	50
16-18	109
10	95
78	178
33	- (tram service still running)

A unidentified 'E/3' car works along Westminster Bridge Road just before the junction with Lambeth Palace Road. The impressive propping on the corner of the New Inn is a reminder that, seven years after the war had ended, much bomb damage remained. Route 40 would be one of the last to be abandoned, on 5 July 1952. *Marcus Eavis / Online Transport Archive*

4. Victoria (Vauxhall Bridge Road)
Considerable improvement has been claimed. This can hardly be so as some bus services now turn in the middle of Vauxhall Bridge Road, blocking all traffic by so doing. This was not so in the days of the trams as, although there were often several trams waiting to enter the terminus, the rest of the road was free for other traffic.

5. Embankment
Traffic congestion has increased since the introduction of buses. Formerly, all public transport was virtually segregated from other traffic. There have been at least two serious accidents due to the conversion.

6. Kingsway Subway
The full effect in Kingsway cannot be judged until the withdrawal of tram routes 33-35 in April. Despite several questions, no authority has yet explained how closing the subway can improve traffic conditions in this part of London.

From the foregoing it will be seen that:

- The improvement in traffic conditions due to withdrawal of the trams is generally negligible

- The reverse often occurs

- At least £9,000,000 has been spent on the conversion scheme, which will show no long-term good results. The money could have been better spent, with better results, on tramway modernisation.

Before proceeding to discuss the advantages of installing a new rapid transit tramway system, the effects of the conversion on services should be mentioned. It should be said that the tram services were far from satisfactory. Journeys were often delayed and many cars never reached their destination. The vehicles were often dirty and bad-riding. It is quite true that in many cases the buses are running less erratically and are keeping better to schedule. This has been claimed as a vindication of the scheme, but the following should be borne in mind when considering this aspect:

- Operation of the trams was inefficient. Many tram drivers deliberately went at a slow speed, even when higher speeds were possible. It is doubtful whether any encouragement was given from higher quarters.

- There is no doubt that the trams could have been operated more efficiently, and it is interesting to note that many tram systems operate their cars regularly, frequently and efficiently.

- The London trams were dirty because no-one bothered to clean them, and bad-riding because maintenance was poor.

- No effort was made to put the track into first-class condition. In the circumstances, it was hardly surprising that the trams were unpopular.

- As regards the effect on passengers waiting to board vehicles, the result has been definitely retrospective. Queues have lengthened because the capacity of the routes has, in most cases, dropped considerably.

On top of this, many services have been cut.

The result of the conversion is, therefore, in general, a deterioration of services.

Economics
It has been claimed that the trams in South London were losing £1,000,000 per annum. For 100 miles of route, this is fantastic. It is suggested that, if they were losing this amount of money, the department concerned is inefficient, and the matter should be investigated. Glasgow has the largest tramway system in the country, and although at the moment it is also losing money it is doing so at only a third of the rate in London. (The financial result of the reintroduction of penury. Fares on the Glasgow trams and, in some cases, buses will be watched with interest.)

It was admitted at the Transport Tribunal in 1950 that the increase in fares (which came into effect on 1 October 1950) was not considered unreasonable in view of the cost of the tramway conversion scheme. Now fares are to go up again!

General
Despite the objection of many Londoners to the trams, several quarters have asked for a trial of modern trams. All these requests have been refused by London Transport, which has also turned down all offers to provide a tram for this purpose.

It will be seen that the public have not been allowed to have a say in the matter; it is feared that the authorities have decided that the trams must go, and that the policy must be carried through despite all protests and adverse effects.

It has already been mentioned that the public were not given an opportunity to see a practical demonstration of modern tramways. Despite this, a modernisation plan, based on existing routes, was prepared and submitted to the Executive for their consideration. The plan could not be considered on the grounds that the Executive were committed to the tram-scrapping policy — a rather peculiar statement, since they instigated the scheme.

It is a shame that Alan Watkins did not live to experience Tramlink, which gave the public just the opportunity he sought 'to see a practical demonstration of modern tramways'.

June 1952, one month to go: turning from Marshalsea Road into Southwark Bridge Road on route 46, 'HR/2' car No 1864 passes Goodwin Buildings, an example of social housing from 1888. *Marcus Eavis / Online Transport Archive*

Ex-West Ham Corporation car No 304 works a route 36 service through St George's Circus, with the Duke of Clarence pub in the background. Built *c*1820, this Grade II-listed building is today under threat — as, by the time of this photograph, was the tramway service; it would be withdrawn on 5 July 1952. *Marcus Eavis / Online Transport Archive*

A young boy has just been admonished for touching another ex-West Ham car, No 299, working route 44 outside the Royal Arsenal Gates in Woolwich. The tram is about to swing round into New Road, and this may be on the last day of tramway operation in London, as the car seems to have chalk smudges along its side, many chalk inscriptions being added to cars that day. The low beading on the West Ham cars precluded them from displaying 'LAST TRAM WEEK' posters. *Marcus Eavis / Online Transport Archive*

'E/3' car No 1986 on route 72 negotiates Eltham Green roundabout, a revised track layout to accommodate this having been in operation since it was built in October 1935. The route would be one of the last to be withdrawn, on 5 July 1952. *Marcus Eavis / Online Transport Archive*

10. "Gonna miss the old tram"
London trams on film

The advent of Internet video and the development and popularity of video-sharing websites such as YouTube has made a plethora of historic film footage, both amateur and professional, more widely available to the public gaze. Complementing these is an ever-widening range of documentary film compilations on DVD. Amongst this footage trams — in particular London's trams — feature quite prominently.

The following is a selection of films that feature London trams. The latter also appear in stock footage of London edited into productions made outside the UK, sometimes quite anachronistically. A good example is the US TV sitcom *I Dream of Jeannie* (1965-70), which used to introduce scenes ostensibly filmed in London with colour footage of trams crossing Westminster Bridge!

Horse-Drawn Traffic Viewed From Elevated Position (1898), directed by Charles Goodwin Norton — A film shot from a high vantage-point at the junction of Euston Road and St Pancras Road. Horse-drawn trams, cabs and carts are seen. One tram pulls up opposite the camera; its destination board reads 'Hampstead–Kings X–Moorgate St'.

Panorama of Ealing from a Moving Tram (1901), directed by William Kennedy Laurie Dickson — A short (1min 20sec) journey through Ealing, filmed from the upper deck of a moving tramcar, when they had the streets to themselves!

Trackless Tramcar (1912), the Topical Film Co — A brief (40sec) fragment of film showing a 'trackless tram car' (trolleybus) being demonstrated at a municipal tramways conference in West Ham.

One Way of Solving Traffic Problem! (1923), the Topical Film Co — An ironic title for a short (1min 10sec) film showing London's tramway and busmen on strike.

'London's Contrasts' (1924), directed by Harry B. Parkinson for Graham-Wilcox Productions — one of a 20-part series called *Wonderful London* (1924), travelogues that captured a fascinating and complex portrait of London in the mid-1920s. The opening sequence of this 11min 53sec instalment features trams in traffic.

Tram's Birthday (1925), British Pathé — West Ham Corporation celebrates the coming-of-age of its tram system in a short (59sec) film which includes shots of a special illuminated tram. Released 2 March 1925.

Lord Mayor Tram Driver (1925), British Pathé — The Lord Mayor, Col Sir William Robert Pryke, steers the first tram (No 1847) over Southwark Bridge, in a 38sec film marking the opening of a new service into the City of London. Released 20 July 1925.

Travel The Cheap Way — By Tramway (1925), produced for West Ham Corporation — Behind the scenes at West Ham tram depot; a row of trams outside the depot; men working in store room; handing equipment over the counter; in the smith's shop; men working around a forge; a pneumatic hammer shown in action with three men hammering some hot metal manually; finally, a man operating machine for boring steel tyres.

London's Buses and Trams (1925), produced by Castle Films in the USA — A travelogue of London featuring famous streets and showing different forms of transport, including trams.

The Open Road (1926), directed by Claude Friese-Greene — Pioneering colour travelogue of a journey through the UK which ends in London and includes a shot of an LCC 'E/1' car turning from Tower Bridge Road into Tooley Street. Friese-Greene was the son of the film pioneer William Friese-Greene, who was portrayed by Robert Donat in the Festival of Britain feature film *The Magic Box* (1951).

The Super Washer (1928), British Pathé — A film of 1min 51sec featuring the LCC's new tram-washing system and showing trams being washed and vacuumed inside. Released 12 March 1928.

Service (1931), London United Tramways — A 15min film showing the construction and introduction of the 'Feltham' tramcars which also shows older classes of tramcar being withdrawn and scrapped.

Linking up London (1931), British Pathé — 2min 4sec showing the inauguration of the LCC's new double-deck 'Pullman' service through the Kingsway Subway. Released 15 January 1931, this is rare footage with synchronous sound of trams in the subway.

Twickenham to Teddington by Trolleybus (1931), London United Tramways — Film of the first day of trolleybus operation (16 May 1931) which includes shots of older classes of tramcar in service.

Love on Wheels (1932), directed by Victor Saville — A musical romance about two people's daily commute on a Green Line coach, which includes shots of Metropolitan trams, including 'Felthams'.

London Life (c1934), British Movietone News — A 1min snippet which opens with a horse-drawn Express Dairies cart on Southampton Row passing as an 'E/3' car lravess the Kingsway Subway. Dated to 1930, the footage indicates a later date.

A Ride over Westminster Bridge (c1936), unknown — Film following a cyclist's progress over Westminster Bridge and along Westminster Bridge Road as far as its junction with Kennington Road. It runs for 2min 32sec and shows eight 'E/1' and 'E/3' cars on routes 16, 35, 24, 26, 33 and 4. The only cars identifiable are 'E/3' No 1998 on route 33 and 'E/1' No 1799 on route 4. The fluidity and speed of the tramway service shines through. It is also good to see clean, well-maintained, un-vestibuled cars without headlamp masks.

The Green Cockatoo (1937), directed by William Cameron Menzies — A mystery thriller that includes a shot of a tram working route 25.

Glimpses of Leytonstone (1938), filmed by Ronald Redburn — Amateur colour film (4min 47sec) depicting everyday street scenes in Leytonstone, including crisply painted and gold-lined cars on route 61 in Leytonstone High Road and at Whipps Cross. Trolleybuses replaced trams on the route on 5 November 1939.

The Londoners (1939), directed by John Taylor for the Realist Film Unit and the LCC — A film, made to celebrate the LCC's Jubilee, which attempted to show the progress of the work of the Council since its inception in 1886; it includes scenes of trams entering the Kingsway Subway in Southampton Row.

The Black Sheep of Whitehall (1941), directed by Basil Dearden — A professor discovers a Nazi plot; there are scenes of a tram working route 72 on Westminster Bridge.

Ordinary People (1941), directed by Jack Lee and J. B. Holmes — Wartime documentary for Britain's allies abroad to show how ordinary people were living in the Blitz. It includes a shot of a tram with most of the side windows boarded up.

This Happy Breed (1944), directed by David Lean — The life of a family between the wars, which features scenes of trams on the Embankment in the background to one scene.

Waterloo Road (1944), directed by Sidney Gilliat — The story of an absconding soldier, which includes shots of trams in wartime livery behind Waterloo station.

Moving Millions (1947), directed by Noel Arthur (Crown Film Unit) for London Transport — Shows the problems involved in the transport of London's millions and how London Transport deals with it; trams are featured. Made on the eve of

the undertaking's becoming part of the nationalised transport system, the film includes a shot of an 'E/3' car working route 31 in the City.

London Belongs to Me (1948), directed by Sidney Gilliat — On 13 March 1948 a sequence set on the lower deck of an 'E/1' car was filmed between Balham and Clapham South, but unfortunately this was cut from the final film, and the footage has been lost! Only glimpses of trams remain.

Passport to Pimlico (1949), directed by Henry Cornelius for Ealing Studios — Despite its title, the film was shot not in Pimlico but a mile away on a set built just off Lambeth Road. The background features trams passing by throughout the film, especially at one point when the action moves into the road.

All Change (1950) (Cine Gazette No 8), London Transport — The last of the Cine Gazette newsreel-style films produced by London Transport before their production was transferred to British Transport Films. Around six of the film's 10 minutes were devoted to the first stage of the replacement of trams with RT buses.

Pool of London (1950), directed by Basil Dearden for Ealing Studios — Producer Michael Relph deliberately included two scenes featuring trams because he had learned of their impending withdrawal and wanted to have a record of them. The first is after seven minutes and shows actor Leslie Phillips aboard a car, later shown to be Class E/1 No 599 on route 70, probably filmed in Tooley Street. The second is after 53 minutes and shows actress Susan Shaw and actor Earl Cameron aboard a tram, which is again revealed to be car 599! Shaw remarks to Cameron: "There won't be any trams soon — they're scrapping them all," to which Cameron replies: "My last tram ride then too," later remarking "Gonna miss the old tram". Just after an hour into the film there is also a scene filmed outside the old Camberwell Palace (now also long gone) of trams on route 58 passing along Denmark Hill at night.

Transport (1950), directed by Peter Bradford — Sponsored by the British Transport Commission, the film tells the story of the development of canals, railways and road transport services in the UK and their subsequent reorganisation and nationalisation in 1948. It includes a shot of an 'E/1' on route 12.

Bus and Tram Graveyard (aka Disposal of Old Buses) (1950), British Pathé — 3min showing the scrapping process in some detail, with synchronous sound. Rare footage.

A Tram-Ride to the Past (1951), British Pathé — 1min 57sec showing the last tram between Tooting and Balham. Includes the same Sunderland and Leeds archive footage as used in *The Elephant Will Never Forget*. Released 11 January 1951.

Dodging the Column (1952), directed by Michael Orrum for British Transport Films — A 132ft distillation column is transported 500 miles by road from Greenwich to Grangemouth. It includes shots of trams in Greenwich.

London's Farewell to its Trams (1952), BBC Television Newsreel — A 2min 47sec newsreel showing trams in New Cross, on the Embankment and the Last Tram ceremony — what *The Elephant Will Never Forget* was meant to be! First screened 6 July 1952.

London's Last Tram (1952), British Pathé — 55sec showing trams running at New Cross and Westminster, the last private tram and the last tram ceremony at New Cross depot. Released 10 July 1952

London Trams make their Final Journey (1952), Gaumont British News: 1min 17sec showing the last cars on route 40 working to New Cross depot on 5 July 1952 and the last tram ceremony there.

Operating London (1952/3), British Transport Films — Edited salvaged footage from an aborted production showing the integrated transport system in London and in which trams feature briefly.

London's trams may have vanished from the streets in July 1952, but some of their paraphernalia continued to feature in films. Notable examples are:

Genevieve (1953), directed by Henry Cornelius for Sirius Productions — Centred on the friendly rivalry between two entrants in the annual London–Brighton car run, their race to be

the first to cross Westminster Bridge is delayed by road works to remove tramlines and ends in victory for 'Genevieve' when the wheels of the other car get jammed in the tramlines whilst taking a short-cut along Lambeth Palace Road, sweeping it round the curve the wrong way into Westminster Bridge Road!

Road under the Strand (1964), British Pathé — 1min 21sec showing completion of the work to form the Strand Underpass using part of the former Kingsway tramway subway. Released 23 January 1964.

Portions of the Kingsway Subway have also featured in a number of films, the first being *Bhowani Junction* (1956), starring Stewart Granger, in which it doubled for a railway tunnel. More recently scenes for the following productions have also utilised the subway: *Hidden City* (1987), *The Avengers* (1988) and *The Escapist* (2008).

It is always worth seeking out and watching documentary and feature films made in the years up to 1952 for glimpses of and scenes featuring London trams.

11. The Elephant's 'other' memory
Another side to the making of *The Elephant Will Never Forget*

The last days of tramway operation were filmed for London Transport by British Transport Films (BTF), and the resultant record was released as London Transport Cine Gazette No 12, better known as *The Elephant Will Never Forget*. Now lauded both as a moving record of the end of an era and as an exemplary piece of filmmaking, ever since its production the film has been the subject of some controversy. The greatest divergence of opinion was between the Head of Production at BTF, the late Edgar Anstey, and the film's director, John Krish. Anstey's view, previously expressed, was that he'd been 'informed in the usual way that the last tram was due to run' and that he'd 'had an idea that this might be a nostalgic thing to do and so talked to John Krish about it'. Together, they 'brainstormed' the idea for the film, which Krish was then dispatched to make because Anstey regarded him as being 'the perfect person for that, he had a romantic approach which suited the material well'.

This is not how John Krish remembers things and he put his side of the circumstances under which *The Elephant Will Never Forget* was made when Patrick Russell interviewed him at an evening screening of his work at the National Film Theatre on 27 May 2003:

Patrick Russell: '… let's move on to British Transport Films — an even more famous centre of documentary-film-making. What's the story there?'

John Krish: 'You mean how did it start?'

Patrick Russell: 'How did it start, and how did you find British Transport Films as a place to work?'

John Krish: 'It started just at the point when a whole lot of other units were closing due to lack of sponsors, and the war was over so the Crown Film Unit closed. British Transport, having just happened because of nationalisation, had a huge pot of money and a huge number of subjects, but the pot of money wasn't really related to what *we* were being paid, I seem to remember. We started very modestly, in two rooms in the headquarters of London Transport, and the feeling was wonderful as this really did seem as if it was going to be a wonderfully exciting new unit.

'I made with Jack Holmes — who had been in the Crown Film Unit as a senior director and was a very lovely man — their fourth production, *This Year — London* [1951], which was about a factory outing, a shoe factory coming from Leicester to London for the day. I think it's a very jolly, simple film that works. … Then they moved to Savile Row and everything changed. We all had offices, and it was not like being

John Krish at the National Film Theatre on 27 May 2003. *British Film Institute*

in a film unit at all. It was like being in a ministry of a film unit. It was dreadful. The producer had a three-bar electric fire and a fitted carpet. The production manager had a two-bar electric fire and a carpet. Jack Holmes and I, who shared an office, had a radiator, and there was even a tea lady! All the atmosphere had gone. Jack Holmes left, and I made *The Elephant Will Never Forget* [1953]. Are we coming to that later?'

Patrick Russell: 'We're coming to that very soon, so tell us the story.'

John Krish: 'In 1952 the trams in London were coming to an end, and I was ordered to go to the New Cross depot on Saturday night with five minutes of film to photograph the chairman of London Transport shaking hands with the driver of the last tram.

(Audience laughs.) I said to [producer] Edgar Anstey, 'There has to be a film here about London's last tram.' And he said, 'There isn't.' (Audience laughs.) And that was that. So I came out of his office determined to make one. I teamed up with Bob Paynter — who … was an assistant cameraman there. Between us and a sympathetic associate producer, we stole film stock from the cupboard, and in those last five days, we made this film without a script. It was a very strange arrangement because the unit knew we were doing it and yet they didn't own up to it. The production manager was so strongly 'in favour of' the film that he didn't allow us any transport! We went to New Cross on a sodding bus, with a camera and a tripod! Well, that was alright. But with Bob Paynter, and Claude Hudson — who was the most wonderful assistant I've ever had — and Bob Paynter's assistant, we just worked our guts off and made this film.

I had no preconception about how it should be, but I did know that I wanted an old couple taking their last tram ride in London before it all finished. I went to a Darby & Joan Club in Lewisham and found a couple. I made sure that they weren't married because I didn't want them sitting in silence throughout the whole trip (audience laughs), and so we shot.

'On the very last night I wanted a shot of the 'last tram' going over Blackfriars Bridge with no traffic on the bridge, just the tram going away from camera. Technically, it was very difficult because it was night and in those days we had no hypersensitive stock. The tram had to go very, very slowly and we had to turn the camera very slowly in order to get an exposure. So there couldn't be any other traffic on the bridge, otherwise it would be [appear to be] going like mad. So we had to have an elaborate signalling system with the police, whose permission we had got to empty the bridge of traffic. We had Claude and the City of London policeman, who was going to be on the brow of Blackfriars Bridge, making sure no traffic was coming towards the camera. I had one [lookout] on my side, making sure no traffic was coming from behind camera. Claude worked out a very complicated signalling process. He said to this City of London policeman: 'You stand on the brow of the bridge. When I flash once, it means we're ready and you flash me back. When I flash you twice, you flash me twice and you are telling me it means the traffic has stopped. When I flash you three times,' Claude says, 'that means we are rolling, the camera's going now. Is that clear? Any problems?' And the City of London policeman said 'Yes, I don't have a torch.' (Audience laughs.) So it was handkerchief time — but we got the shot.

' When the film had been cut, I had by chance a collection of old music-hall songs — because in the army I had done an old music hall show regularly. I came across a song about the tram called 'Riding on Top of the Car' and Edward Williams did a wonderful arrangement of it. I got the Darby & Joan Club and Archie Harradine from the Players Theatre to sing the track you will hear. We had a sing-song at the Darby & Joan Club; we gave them tea, there were song sheets, and there was a band. They sang the song I needed, but when I got back to the cutting room I discovered something really dreadful. When I was setting it up, I said to the production manager at British Transport —who was against the film, remember — that I wanted Ken Cameron, the old Crown Film Unit sound-recordist to do it. He said, 'Oh, we can't have Ken, he's too much money.' He was about £5-an-hour more — it was absolute rubbish. So they gave me a 'backstreet abortionist' for a recordist, and when I heard the stuff it was unusable. So we had to do it all over again for the sake of £10 or £20. By the time that we did it, it was already winter and I was asking very old people — like me now, of course — to turn out and come to the club for another sing-song, and Edward had to bring the band back. It was awful to have to do it again but the spirit of the thing was almost the same, although not quite in my ears.'

(Screening of The Elephant Will Never Forget)

John Krish: 'There is, of course, a postscript to this. I was sacked for making that. Edgar Anstey wrote to me — it was just a couple of lines thanking me for all the hard work. I can't remember the lines. Patrick [Russell] said I should have framed it. In fact, I tore it up, I was so angry. So Anstey thanked me for all the work I had done but said it was time the unit had 'new blood'. And I was twenty-nine! (Audience laughs.) But it stayed on his conscience until he died, because every time we met he'd say, 'Oh, I must tell you about the tram film. They're holding it in Moscow as a supreme example of British documentary. They love our film.' Our film? Please! (Audience laughs.)

John Krish (1923-) worked as a writer-director from 1948 to 1985 and directed short films for a large number of organisations, including British Transport Films, the National Coal Board, the General Post Office, the National Union of Teachers, various charities, including the NSPCC, and the Central Office of Information. He also directed feature films, including Unearthly Stranger (1963) and episodes of TV programmes, notably The Saint and The Avengers, for which he also directed the famous stylish opening credits, plus numerous

advertisements. Going against the grain cost him his career with BTF; he did make one more film for the organisation, *The Finishing Line* (1977), but only *after* Edgar Anstey had retired.

A lot of what John Krish said in his interview with Patrick Russell in 2003 is borne out by the film's log, which was production No 108 in BTF history and given the working title 'Trams'. This is reproduced here for the first time. The term 'Roll' refers to the film loaded into the camera. A typical movie camera roll would hold around 400ft of cine film, giving a filming time of around 4½ minutes. The term 'Slate' refers to the 'clapperboard' device used in the film industry to identify each scene as it is filmed. When John Krish was directing *The Elephant Will Never Forget* the main body of these was formed by a piece of slate upon which the roll number, scene number, date and director's name would be chalked — hence the term 'slate'. With these details chalked on, the clapperboard would be held in view of the camera before filming began on a scene and a hinged piece of wood on its top would be brought into sharp contact with the main body of the slate's frame to produce a sharp, loud 'clap' — hence clapperboard. Once processed, these clapperboard images were the only way of identifying individual scenes on the film — the 'clap' sound also being the initial means of synchronising the images filmed with the sound recorded at the same time.

Roll 1: 4 April 1952

Slate	Description
01	Trams entering Kingsway Tunnel
02	Ditto
03	Ditto — end
04	Kingsway Tunnel — people walking down steps
05	Tram entering into Kingsway Tunnel
06	Tram coming out of Kingsway Tunnel
07	Tram passing from R to L along Embankment passing Sphinx Statue
08	Tram coming out of Embankment entrance of Kingsway Tunnel
09	Top shot — tram going round Embankment
10	Embankment from Westminster Bridge
11	Embankment — tram stops at stop — and moves off
12	Medium shot — passengers getting off tram
13	Long shot — looking south over Westminster Bridge
14	Tram comes around corner by Boadicea statue

Roll 2: 8 April 1952

Slate	Description
01	*(no record)*
02	Closing of Kingsway Tunnel
03	Ditto

Roll 3: 1 July 1952

Slate	Description
01	Medium shot — New Cross depot — tram — wheel
02	Tram R to L — 'London's Last Tram' poster — no good
03	Travelling in tram coming out of depot — no good
04	Pan from L to R across static trams — no good
05	Ditto — OK
06	Long shot — Siemens chimney in background — trams coming and going
07	Long shot — night — Elephant & Castle

Roll 4: 1 July 1952

Slate	Description
01	Medium long shot — dusk — African visitor to London on Westminster Bridge
02	Dusk — Trams going past Boadicea's statue — Westminster Bridge
03	Long shot — pan with trams to gasworks — Old Kent Road — no goo
04	Ditto — Take 2 — dusk — OK
05	Tram coming towards camera — dusk — sunlight on tram lines

At least six trams (and one trolleybus) feature in this view of Woolwich change-pit during Last Tram Week. The conductor of 'E/3' car No 183 swings the trolley boom as No 100 (ex East Ham No 70) moves through to shed its plough.
D. W. K. Jones / Online Transport Archive

Roll 5: 2 July 1952

Slate	Description
01	Dull light — Old Kent Road — interior of tram from conductor's end — tram handle in foreground — looking back as another tram approaches stop
02	Pigeons on tram track — no good
03	Top shot — looking down on driver
04-06	Ditto
07	Along Westminster Bridge — Big Ben — tram coming towards camera
08	Driver looking right — tram travelling
09	Driver's foot on alarm bell
10	Travelling out of New Cross depot — retake of set-up in Roll 3
11	Interior — tram — travelling — New Cross Street and St George's Road — medium shot — tram starts and stops
12	Interior of tram — looking towards road — hand on brake coming in and out of picture
13	Interior of tram — onto street — driver in foreground — Deptford to New Cross — Marquis of Granby pub
14	Ditto — shot from top deck
15	Shot from top deck — travelling past power station at Deptford, Greenwich Road
16	'Annandale School Says Thank You to London Trams' poster — taken from interior top of tram
17	Retake of set-up Roll 3 — 'London's Last Tram' poster
18	Long shot — New Cross depot — new building left — trams moving in background
19	Entrance New Cross depot — trams moving in and out — weather dull — no good
20-21	Ditto — no good
22	Ditto
23	Top shot — Westminster Bridge
24	Exterior night — tram around corner R to L
25	Tram across Blackfriars Bridge — too fast — night — no good
26	Retake — OK — tram around curve R to L — night

Roll 6: 3 July 1952

Slate	Description
01	Exterior — raining — Woolwich — factory workers boarding trams
02	Ditto
03	Outside Siemens Woolwich Works
04	Ditto
05	Outside Siemens Works
06	Ditto
07	Woolwich
08	Woolwich — rain — tram coming towards camera
09	Plough leaves tram and comes towards camera
10	Tram towards camera through puddle — no good
11	Ditto — OK
12	Tram across Blackfriars Bridge (retake of set-up Roll 5)
13	Camera test
14	Night — Embankment from Blackfriars Bridge towards Westminster Bridge — trams towards camera
15	Embankment tram R to L — tram stops and starts
16	Ditto
17	Camera test

Roll 7: 4 July 1952

Slate	Description
01	Insert — tramlines — Free Ferry via Woolwich Road
02	Savoy Street — Strand — via Brockley — Old Kent Road
03	City and Southwark via Old Kent Road
04	Ditto
05	Ditto — tram moves into camera
06	Westminster
07	Westminster — tram moves away — no good
08	2nd take — ditto
09	Man putting the sign on side of tram 'boarding up' — action poor — no good
10	2nd take — ditto — OK
11	Foot on alarm bell (soft focus) — no good
12	Camera on ground — tram cow-catcher — tram towards camera — no good
13	Ditto — OK

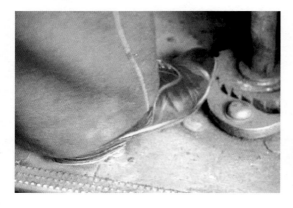

Roll 5, filmed on 2 July 1952, included most of the close-up shots of tram drivers and the controls and operation of trams, such as this one of a driver's foot releasing the ratchet on the hand brake. *British Film Institute*

14	Medium shot — interior of tram top deck — 'Darby' and 'Joan' sitting in centre — Old Kent Road
15	Medium-close shot — 'Darby' and 'Joan' — Old Kent Road — interior of tram
16	Close-up — 'Joan'
17	Close-up — 'Joan'
18	'Darby' sitting in tram
19	Conductor upstairs taking fares from 'Darby' and 'Joan'
20	Tram interior — 'Darby' and 'Joan' foreground and going over Blackfriars Bridge

Roll 8: 4 July 1952

Slate	Description
01	Close-up (interior) conductor of tram
02	Three shots — 'Darby' and 'Joan' and conductor walk out of shot right
03	Close-up — 'Joan' talking to conductor — off screen
04	Medium shot — New Cross Street — tram comes towards camera
05	Inspector timing trams New Cross Street
06-07	Ditto
08	New Cross Street — panned shot with trams passing R to L
09	Medium close shot — inspector
10	Interior of tram — travelling shot on Embankment — shot from top deck
11-13	Ditto

The people who were said to miss the trams most were the Cockneys. In the film they were represented by an elderly couple. John Krish explained: 'I went to a Darby & Joan club in Lewisham and found a couple. I made sure that they weren't married, because I didn't want them sitting in silence throughout the whole trip.' *British Film Institute*

John Krish wanted a shot of a tram going over Blackfriars Bridge at night with no other traffic about. Having failed to get the shot the previous night, they tried again on 3 July 1952, with more success. John Krish explained that 'the tram had to go very, very slowly, and we had to turn the camera very slowly in order to get an exposure'. *British Film Institute*

14	Interior of tram — two shots 'Darby' and 'Joan' — river in background — 'Joan' waves
15	Travelling shot along Embankment — Festival Hall
16	Interior of tram — Embankment — passing river launch — etc, etc.
17	Two shots — 'Darby' and 'Joan' — conductor comes into picture — fares are paid
18-19	Ditto
20	New Cross Street — tram over points outside depot
21	Ditto
22	Man on points — trams in background
23-25	Ditto
26	Interior of tram — lower deck — conductor switches on light — no good
27	Ditto — OK
28	Long shot — interior of tram — people taking their seats — top deck — tram moves off
29	Long shot — interior of tram — conductor taking fares and man with two children
30	Four shots of two passengers — leave tram — (against light)
31	Four shots facing light (tram swaying)
32	Three shots — side angle — of children
33	Children talking to women
34	Child and father taking seat in front of 'Darby' and 'Joan' (Take 1)
35	Ditto (Take 2)
36	Facing 'engine' — couple in foreground — man has his arm around girl

Roll 9: 5 July 1952

Slate	Description
01	Lower deck — people smoking — lower deck!! (Take 1) — no good
02	Lower deck facing driver — conductor comes through door
03	From driver's end, looking at passengers — passengers boarding tram
04	Lower deck — travelling shot
05	Lower deck — conductor collecting fares — passengers getting up to get off
06	Small boy moves down to empty seat in front of friend — conductor taking fares
07	Medium shot — small boys in left of screen 'tram-spotters'
08	Close shot — boy onto notebook
09	Close shot — book
10-14	Ditto
15	Top shot looking downstairs — conductor comes up stairs (conductor's end)
16	Ditto — goes downstairs (driver's end)
17	Top shot — tram starts — conductor climbs stairs
18	Taken from inside car (BTC Humber) — people climbing aboard tram
19	Ditto
20	Top shot — Woolwich Market — pawnbrokers' balls in foreground — lift up to long shot of market
21	Woolwich — ploughing sequence — changing over to middle rail and centre to overhead — rail near to Free Ferry
22-34	Ditto

35	Tying up overhead cord — no good for action
36	Ditto
37-43	Ditto
44	Long shot — Embankment — Big Ben in background — tram moves away from camera — no good
45	Tram goes past St Paul's Cathedral
46	Ditto

Roll 10: 5 July 1952

Slate	Description
01	Saturday-night ceremony — Chairman and group waiting for Last Tram
02	Long shot — Last Tram — fireworks, etc, etc
03	Chairman and group
04	Last Tram coming into depot
05	Ditto
06	Last Tram coming up to stop
07	Chairman shaking hands with driver
08	Ditto
09	Chairman and group await Last Tram
10	People leaning out of top deck of tram watching ceremony
11	Pan L to R past crowd to group
12	Penultimate (This material not to be cut — shot for record purposes only) [All this material shot from top position]

An 'E/3' car from the 161-210 series working a route 40 service along the Embankment on 5 July 1952. To the right another photographer is on hand to immortalise the event. *Online Transport Archive*

A line of three be-chalked cars at New Cross Gate on 5 July 1952, headed by E/3 No 200. To the right a man is pointing out the significance of the occasion to his grandson. *N Hamshere / Online Transport Archive*

Attended by crowds and lit by a flare from the upper deck, one of London's very last trams makes its stately progress towards New Cross depot. *Online Transport Archive*

Filming of the Last Tram ceremony at New Cross depot was marred somewhat by the fact that one roll of film — No 11 — was scratched and out of focus. Luckily the footage shot by the other camera covering the event was fine. Here London Transport Chairman Lord Latham has just given his 'Farewell Old Tram' speech. *British Film Institute*

An extract from the log for 'Trams Prod: 108', detailing some of the shots taken of the Last Tram ceremony, at New Cross depot in the early hours of 6 July 1952.
London Transport Museum

13	Chairman and mayors climb off tram
14-16	Ditto
17	Last Tram ceremony — Chairman and group
18	Ditto
19	(Soft focus) — medium shot — Chairman making speech — no good
20	Men hanging onto top of tram watching ceremony
21	Penultimate tram — shot from ground (2ndcamera)
22-23	Ditto
24	Tram conductor towards camera (2nd camera)
25	Pan with Last Tram to stopping position
26	Group milling around Last Tram
27	Pan L to R with group
28	Shots of crowds milling
29	Ditto
30	People leaning out of top of tram — pan onto group
31	Ditto — pan L to R
32	People leaning out of top of tram
33	Ditto
34	Top shot of ceremony — pan across crowd (1st camera position)
35	Ditto
36	Group chatting
37	Group signing autographs
38	Ditto
39	Inspectors, drivers and conductors around tram
40	Group milling around tram
41	Close group — drivers talking to conductors — tramcars off in background
42	Group looks at camera
43-44	Ditto
45	Group of lady conductors
46	Dead trams in depot

Roll 11: 5 July 1952
No good — scratches and focus

Roll 12: 9 July 1952

Slate	*Description*
01-03	'Tram Stop' signs

Roll 13: 11 July 1952

Slate	*Description*
01-02	'Last Tram' poster — tram bell being pushed

Roll 14: 1 September 1952

Slate	*Description*
01-12	Charlton — break-up of London's last trams

Roll 15: 21 February 1953

Slate	*Description*
01-02	Elephant & Castle — Elephant & Castle inn sign

The Elephant & Castle inn sign was filmed on 21 February 1953 and provided the backdrop to the title frame for the film, which up to this point had been called simply *Trams*. *British Film Institute*

The last page of the narration script for *The Elephant Will Never Forget*, which Brewster Mason recorded on 27 March 1953. The very last line was omitted. *London Transport Museum*

Post-production work on the film took place between 15 August 1952 and 19 May 1953. Brewster Mason's narration was recorded on 27 March 1953.

The above log gives a number of insights into the production of *The Elephant Will Never Forget* and also confirms much of what John Krish had to say about his experiences working on the film:

Rolls 1 and 2 show that some film record had been made of the Kingsway Subway in April 1952, three months before work began on 'Trams'.

John Krish's remark that he 'was ordered to go to the New Cross depot on Saturday night with five minutes of film to photograph the Chairman of London Transport shaking hands with the driver of the last tram' is supported by the note against Roll 10, slate 12: 'Penultimate (This material not to be cut — shot for record purposes only).'

On the last day the trams were withdrawn progressively. Here 'E/3' car No 1974 pulls into Penhall Road scrapyard as a breakdown tender waits behind, lest any car should require 'assistance'. *C. Carter / Online Transport Archive*

The bulk of the filming, on Rolls 4-11 above, was done between 1 and 5 July 1952, which squares with John Krish's remark that '… in those last five days we made this film without a script'.

The overall nine-month post-production period for the film also tallies with John Krish's comments about having to redo the sound recordings of the music-hall songs. Indeed, the production log shows that the first attempt at this was made on 16 December 1952, and 'No Good' is marked against the recordings. Krish also said of the re-recording that 'By the time that we did it, it was already winter…' — the actual date was 31 March 1953.

Finally, the fact that the Elephant & Castle Inn sign was filmed on 21 February 1953, some 4½ months after principal filming ended, suggests that the film was given its now famous title only at this latter date.

As with the films described in the previous chapter, it is possible to view *The Elephant Will Never Forget* online, notably on London's Transport Museum website at www.ltmcollection.org/films/index

The scene just inside the gates at Penhall Road scrapyard, also known as the 'Tramatorium'. 'E/3' No 1930 sheds its plough for the very last time. *D. W. K. Jones / Online Transport Archive*

London's last trams were broken up at Penhall Road between July 1952 and January 1953 by George Cohen (600 Group) Ltd, which firm's workers are seen watching as a steel hawser attached to the back of a tractor pulls the body of 'E/3' car No 1940 off its bogies. *D. W. K. Jones / Online Transport Archive*

Said hawser can be seen dangling from the rear of the tractor parked to the left of this impressive line-up of 20 of the 26 lines of cars which led off the traverser, the pit for which fills the foreground. *Marcus Eavis / Online Transport Archive*

12. Jams beat trams
The legacy of Croydon Tramlink

One of the slogans used to promote Croydon Tramlink ahead of its inauguration was 'Trams Beat Jams'. Ten years on, so far as both the Croydon system and the future of trams in London are concerned, it is tempting to say that 'jams beat trams'!

Further tram links
Tramlink's success was immediate and has never been in doubt. Ridership reached over 16,000,000 per year after the first year of operation of the existing system. As early as 2001 the Mayor of London was seeking initial views on the viability of a number of extensions to the system for consideration from the summer of 2002. The possible routes chosen were:

- Sutton Town Centre/Station–St Helier–Morden– Morden Road–Wimbledon and also Croydon (including via St Helier Hospital and direct routes and routeing variants within Sutton town centre);

- Sutton–St Helier–Mitcham–Tooting (including routeing variants direct and via Mitcham Junction);

- Mitcham Junction–Mitcham town centre;

- Central Croydon–Purley/Purley Station–Coulsdon);

  Central Croydon–Thornton Heath–Norbury– Streatham, and;

- Harrington Road/Beckenham Junction–Crystal Palace (various route options)

From these one clear 'candidate' emerged — an extension to Crystal Palace from the system's existing Harrington Road tram stop — a 3km (1.8-mile) route that would cut the journey time from Croydon to Crystal Palace to 18 minutes and provide an interchange with the extended East London line at Crystal Palace station.

Croydon Tramlink No 2541 approaches East Croydon station on 31 August 2003. When introduced the trams wore a livery based on that of the former London trams and were numbered in sequence following on from the highest-numbered car in the former fleet. *Author*

Croydon Tramlink No 2544 enters Pitlake Street from George Street in Croydon and passes Whitgift Hospital, founded 1596. *Author*

Moments later the formation descends the slope into Pitlake Street — a striking modern contrast to Whitgift Hospital and the older properties in George Street behind. *Author*

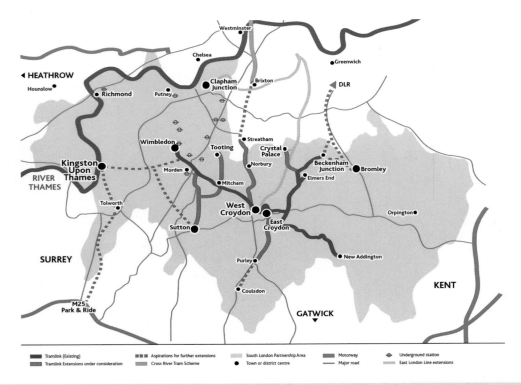

Some of the possible extensions to the Croydon Tramlink system that were considered back in 2002. *Author's collection*

An extension to Crystal Palace emerged as the preferred option for extending Croydon Tramlink. This is the route that was chosen and upon which consultation was held. *Author's collection*

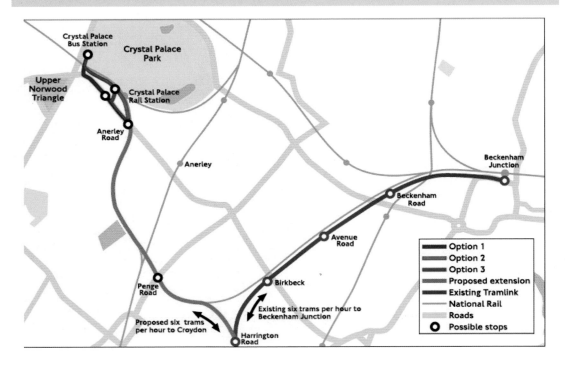

The route would have two stops — on Penge Road and Anerley Road — and terminate at Crystal Palace bus station, but between the latter and Anerley Road three route options were proposed:

- on street along Anerley Hill;

- from Anerley Road on lines parallel to Network Rail past Crystal Palace station, then along Ledrington Road to Crystal Palace Park, then parallel to Anerley Hill in a cutting on the Park periphery before climbing an embankment to terminate next to the bus station;

- along Ledrington Road and then as Option 2.

From 19 October to 18 December 2006, Transport for London (TfL) asked the public for views on these route options. A total of 1,520 responses were received and 67% showed a clear preference for option 2, many citing that it would have the least impact on traffic and provide good interchange with Crystal Palace railway station. On 8 June 2007 TfL announced that a route for the extension would be decided towards the end of 2007. Prospects seemed good as, in addition to this public support, 78% of the local residents most affected by the scheme were in favour of it; the boroughs of Croydon and Bromley reaffirmed their commitment to the project, and a petition was received from 75 businesses in Crystal Palace supporting the extension. Things augured well for the Crystal Palace extension, but an election for the Mayor of London loomed on the horizon in May 2008.

Early in 2007 Tramlink also lost one of its greatest advocates. Stephen Parascandolo, a young and gifted signalling engineer who had started the unofficial but highly informative croydon-tramlink.co.uk website as a schoolboy and remained its webmaster, died in a car accident on 7 February 2007 aged 26. In recognition of his contribution to the success of the scheme, Tramlink named a tram in his honour on 20 October 2007. Back in 2001 Stephen kindly allowed this author to use material from his website in an earlier book on this subject. Upon seeing his words in print he commented that: 'It was a delight to see the history making events recorded on my site make it into print for future reference.'

Anerley Road to Crystal Palace Parade: route details

Option 1:
Anerley Hill (on-street)

The tram route joins Anerley Road slightly to the north of the railway bridge. The route continues along Anerley Road to the junction with Anerley Vale and Brunswick Place.

There would be a tram stop on Anerley Road near this junction, and another possible stop near the Anerley Road bridge over the railway line.

The tram would then continue up Anerley Hill, cross into Crystal Palace Park just north of the Brunel Tower base and terminate right next to the bus terminus on Crystal Palace Parade.

We would need to move the bus stop to the north of the railway bridge. Parking spaces and loading bays on Anerley Road may also need to be moved to accommodate the tram. Initial assessments suggest that the tram would not

have a substantial impact on traffic when running along Anerley Hill. The tramway would be designed to fit in with the Anerley Road Conservation Area.

Main benefits:	Main impacts:
• Good interchange with the bus station	• Possible property acquisition
• Good access to Upper Norwood Triangle	• Removal of loading bays and parking spaces on Anerley Road
• Direct access to shops on Anerley Road	• Interchange with Crystal Palace station not ideal, as passengers need to cross a busy road to reach the train station
• Limited impact on Crystal Palace Park	• More traffic disruption during construction than options 2 and 3
	• Reduced reliability due to road traffic

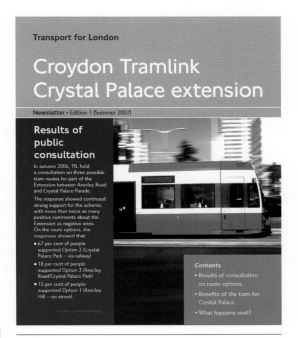

Transport for London

Croydon Tramlink Crystal Palace extension

Newsletter • Edition 1 (Summer 2007)

Results of public consultation

In autumn 2006, TfL held a consultation on three possible tram routes for part of the Extension between Anerley Road and Crystal Palace Parade.

The response showed continued strong support for the scheme, with more than twice as many positive comments as negative ones. On the route options, the responses showed that:

- 67 per cent of people supported Option 2 (Crystal Palace Park – via railway)
- 18 per cent of people supported Option 3 (Anerley Road/Crystal Palace Park)
- 15 per cent of people supported Option 1 (Anerley Hill – on street).

>> story continues inside

Contents
- Results of consultation on route options
- Benefits of the tram for Crystal Palace
- What happens next?

MAYOR OF LONDON

Transport for London

A new London tram system?

The success of Croydon Tramlink inspired others to consider the return of trams to streets elsewhere in London. In total five schemes were proposed that included trams in whole or part. Following on from the development of these schemes there would, almost inevitably, have been further lines proposed to make sensible links between the 'existing' ones, to create a more unified system.

The tram schemes proposed for London in the 2000s were:

City Tram

A 17km (10.5-mile) scheme proposed by the Corporation of London to complement Cross River Tram with a core section from Elephant & Castle up Borough High Street and past London Bridge station, running across London Bridge itself and through the City via Monument station, Gracechurch Street and Bishopsgate, to Liverpool Street station and then to Shoreditch. Here it would have divided into two northern branches:

- Great Eastern Street–Angel–Highbury & Islington

- Shoreditch High St–Hackney Central

There would also have been two southern branches:

- Battersea–Vauxhall–Elephant & Castle (to an interchange with CRT)

- Elephant & Castle–Oval–Stockwell–Brixton.

North London Tram

A tram scheme mooted in the Mayor of London's Question Time on 24 June 2004: 'We are now examining bringing forward proposals for a North London Tram through Enfield and Haringey and so on, so that all the London suburbs will benefit from trams'. It is unclear whether this was developed any further.

Oxford Street Tram

Another scheme suggested by the Mayor of London, this time on 18 September 2006, when plans were outlined to turn Oxford Street into a near traffic-free zone, with just trams running along the street to provide a hop-on service for shoppers. If successful, the 2.4km (1.5-mile) tram service would run from end to end of Oxford Street, with taxis able to cut across from north to south.

Cross River Transit

Proposed from 2002 by the Cross River Partnership, this 16km (10-mile) scheme was for one line — Camden Town–Peckham, via Waterloo and Elephant & Castle — with two branches:

- Euston–King's Cross/St Pancras–King's Cross North

- Waterloo–Kennington–Brixton

Some sections were designed to relieve the most overcrowded stretches of the Underground while others were to provide rail connections in areas which relied on buses. It was envisaged that Cross River Tram would carry 9,000 people per hour in each direction during peak periods.

Transport for London contracted Ipsos MORI to conduct a public consultation on route options for Cross River Transit in September 2007. In its report TfL noted that, in a public consultation in 2002, 92% of respondents had supported the principle of the scheme. In the new consultation a total of 5,065 responses were received during the consultation period, 20 November 2006 – 30 January 2007. These showed the following preferences for the five main sections and their route options:

Section 1:
Euston–Waterloo: one route alignment — 77%

Section 2:
Euston–King's Cross: two route options
    Option 1 (via Crowndale Road and Pancras Road) — 35%
    Option 2 (via Somers Town) — 55%

Section 3:
Euston–Camden Town: two route options
    Option 1 (via Camden High Street) — 65%
    Option 2 (via Bayham Street/Crowndale Road) — 25%

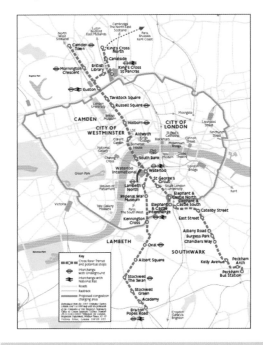

The proposed Cross River Transit system. *Author's collection*

Cross River Transit's proposals also included computer-generated images to show how the scheme might look if built. Here a tram is depicted entering the City over Waterloo Bridge. *Author's collection*

Section 4:
Waterloo–Oval/Brixton:
Waterloo–Oval: two route options
    Option 1 (via Elephant & Castle) — 52%
    Option 2 (via Lambeth North) — 36%
Oval–Brixton: two route options
    Option 1 (via Stockwell) — 34%
    Option 2 (via Brixton Road) — 47%
Brixton town centre: two route options
    Option 1 (via Effra Road) — 53%
    Option 2 (via Canterbury Crescent) — 19%

Section 5:
Waterloo–Peckham: two route options
    Option 1 (via Burgess Park) — 51%
    Option 2 (via Wells Way) — 37%
Peckham town centre: two route options
    Option 1 (via Jocelyn Street/Peckham Arch)
    — 26%
    Option 2 (via Jocelyn Street/north of Peckham
    Library) — 51%
Peckham town centre terminus: two route options
    Option 1 (via Clayton Road) — 32%
    Option 2 (via Cerise Road) — 44%

These routes all contained evocative names recalling
    London's first tram network.

Section Two
Euston to King's Cross

Two route options have been identified for this section which runs between Euston Station and King's Cross.

Both options serve the King's Cross and St Pancras area including the new international rail terminal.

It is important that we have your views on this section. Please complete the questionnaire at the back of this brochure to give us your feedback.

Option 1 - green
Euston to King's Cross via Crowndale Road and Pancras Road

From Euston station the route travels north along Eversholt Street then left into Lidlington Place and right onto Hampstead Road. It then turns right onto Crowndale Road. At the eastern end of Crowndale Road the route crosses into Pancras Road and then left in to Goods Way, approaching King's Cross Station from the north. In the opposite direction, the route turns left out of Crowndale Road to go south along Eversholt Street.

Advantages

- Interchange with Underground at Mornington Crescent
- Access to shops and amenities at Mornington Crescent
- Good access to St. Pancras Hospital

Disadvantages

- Longer and less direct route
- No direct interchange with St Pancras Station

Part of the consultation on Cross River Transit; this page relates to Section 2 (Euston–King's Cross). *Author's collection*

West London Tram

A 19km (12-mile) scheme proposed from 2003 for an on-street light rail line running along the Uxbridge Road corridor in West London, promoted by TfL. The line was designed to run along the congested Uxbridge Road from Uxbridge to Shepherd's Bush serving Hillingdon, Southall, Hanwell, West Ealing, Ealing and Acton en route, and to replace the heavily used 207, 427 and 607 bus services. It was also to have served Brunel University and would have revived a tram route established in 1904, which was replaced by trolleybus route 607, itself superseded by the present bus routes.

Momentum built up behind the last two schemes — on both sides. The 'Pro' lobby included the incumbent Mayor of London and the relevant boroughs; the 'Anti' lobby mustered local residents, traders and politicians to form an able and vociferous group of campaigners. Support and opposition also divided along political lines, the West London Tram scheme coming under the closest scrutiny and the most vehement attack!

The song remains the same

Much of the opposition voiced to the West London Tram scheme has a familiar ring to it, which some, especially those with an eye to history, found familiar.

A map showing the routes chosen for the proposed West London Tram scheme. *Author's collection*

The 'Anti' lobby cited that:

* any plan to introduce a tram along the Uxbridge Road would simply add to congestion rather than reduce it, with cars having to compete for the same amount of road space;

* side streets would effectively become rat-runs;

* there would be much more pollution, congestion, noise and danger to pedestrians, especially children;

* some, maybe all, West Ealing shops on the Uxbridge Road would close down;

* it is not acceptable to route (a large) volume of traffic past people's houses.

Sound familiar? Almost 150 years earlier the good citizens of Marylebone were using much the same arguments against G. F. Train's proposed line, citing that:

* (a certain street) was of insufficient width for a street railway;

* the rails, as laid down, are dangerous, and have caused accidents, besides being an impediment to trade;

  to subject any considerable thoroughfare to a disruption of its pavement, and even the partial stoppage of its traffic, without anything approaching certainty whether the whole would not have to be taken up again, and the old state of the street restored within six months, would be utter folly;

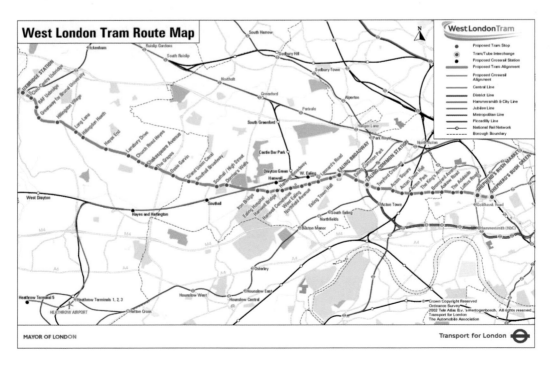

- the scheme would be fraught with the greatest danger to the lives and limbs of the public, and impede the public traffic;

- the adoption of (the scheme) would most seriously injure the interests of the inhabitants, and impede the general traffic of the road.

This is yet another validation of Jean-Baptiste Alphonse Karr's aphorism that *plus ça change, plus c'est la même chose* (the more things change, the more they remain the same).

Cancellation of West London Tram

One consequence of the opposition to West London Tram was a change of political control on Ealing Council after the May 2006 local elections. This was one of the final nails in the scheme's coffin. Transport for London postponed the West London Tram project indefinitely on 2 August 2007. The decision followed the announcement that the central government was to go ahead with the Crossrail project. Opponents of the tramway were critical of the fact that £30 million had already been spent on the project before its cancellation. Transport for London has pledged to work with the local boroughs to increase bus provision instead.

The loss of Mayoral support

Sustaining the remaining tram schemes was the unwavering support of the incumbent Mayor of London, but, as 2008 began, Mayoral elections loomed on the horizon …

The election for London Mayor was held on 1 May 2008; the incumbent lost, and his successor took office on 5 May. This also marked a change of political control, the effects of which were soon seen. On 27 June the ownership and management of Croydon Tramlink was transferred from the concession-holder — Tramtrack Croydon Ltd — to TfL London Rail, in a £98 million deal that terminated a 99-year concession agreement which still had 88 years to run. One reason given for this change was that TfL would save millions in payments to Tramtrack Croydon Ltd, which had amounted to £4 million in 2007 and was expected to increase significantly, had things not changed. A fairly immediate consequence of the transfer of ownership came in October 2008 when the system's name was shortened to 'Tramlink'; worse was to come.

On 11 November 2008 the new Mayor of London announced that the £170 million plan to extend Tramlink to Crystal Palace was to be abandoned, along numerous other transport projects across the capital, together worth more than £3,000 million. Instead the money would be invested in improving the Tube, introducing a new Routemaster bus, and the Crossrail project to build a railway across London. The Mayor added that 'We need to focus on the projects that deliver real benefits for Londoners and let go of those that lack the funding for completion.' Subsequently it was announced that there was funding in TfL's business plan up until 2010 to develop the Tramlink extension to Crystal Palace.

Quickly and unceremoniously, all mention of new tram schemes vanished from TfL's website, to be replaced by a stark message: 'We can't find the page you are looking for' (and on partner websites by: 'This account has been suspended').

One immediate reaction to this news was the start of a petition campaign in support of the Cross River Transit scheme, which was heralded with the slogan: 'Back the Cross River TRAM Boris!' The petition ended with the words: 'We call on the Mayor of London Boris Johnson to confirm his commitment to the Cross River Tram and to do everything in his power to ensure that it is delivered as soon as possible.'

Pro-Cross River Tram protesters prepare to hand in the first round of signatures on their 'Back the Cross River TRAM Boris!' petition late in 2008. *Back the Cross River TRAM Boris!' campaign*

On 5 February 2010 the Mayor of London stated that TfL was committed to increasing the capacity of Tramlink and was working with the London Borough of Croydon to do so. In addition some initial investigation of Tramlink extensions to meet these challenges has been undertaken, and this was to be explored further over the next six months with boroughs and other key stakeholders. This would include a more detailed

assessment of its traffic, environmental and economic impacts with a view to selecting a preferred route, carrying out a detailed design survey and holding a public consultation in preparation for seeking the necessary powers for implementation. The results will be included within the South London sub-regional transport plan, due for completion in late summer 2010. However, within the current business plan period (to 2017/18) there was no funding available for Tramlink extensions, and to progress such a scheme additional funds would have to be sought from Government or other sources. The Mayor of London also declared a continuing commitment to improve the existing Tramlink system. Under consideration were buying or leasing more trams, making the current trams longer, replacing single track with double track, improving the Wimbledon terminus and installing a real-time passenger information system.

Some indication of the Mayor of London's declared 'continuing commitment to improving the existing Tramlink system' was provided by a new standard livery of light green, white and blue, seen here on car No 2544 in George Street, Croydon. *Leewood Projects*

However, by September 2010 mention, at least, of Cross River Tram had reappeared on the TfL website, where the following appeared: 'Proposals to build an on-street tram link running between Euston and Waterloo, with branches to Camden Town and King's Cross in the north, and Brixton and Peckham in the south, are on hold due to constraints on our funding. Future work will now concentrate on working with the boroughs, the London Development Agency and the Greater London Authority to assess potential alternatives to the scheme. Recommendations from the study will form part of a future bid to Government for more funding.'

So, there remains a slender hope of some 'tram tomorrow', but, once again, the words used to conclude *The Elephant Will Never Forget* seem strangely prophetic: '… the next tram had gone'.